Sept. '06.

Ernest,

I hope you enjoy
your daughter Carmi's
story (pg. 79) of how you are a
special in her eyes to marry a
man like you! Now you can know
the real story. I hope you will enjoy
the book.

Susan Schneider

Susan Schneider

Unforgettable
Vignettes of Love

Cold Tree Press
Nashville, Tennessee

Published by Cold Tree Press
Nashville, Tennessee
www.coldtreepress.com

© 2006 Susan Schneider. All rights reserved.
Cover Photograph by Sergei Krasii
Cover Design © 2006 Cold Tree Press
This book may not be reproduced in any form without express written permission.

Library of Congress Control Number: 2006932464

Printed in the United States of America
ISBN 1-58385-095-3

Table of Contents

Introduction & Dedication

chapter one	*Persistence Pays Off*	3
chapter two	*Love at First Sight*	31
chapter three	*Ups and Downs and Ups*	61
chapter four	*Childhood Romances*	89
chapter five	*Parental Involvement*	105
chapter six	*Looking for Mr. and Mrs. Right*	133
chapter seven	*The Female Pursuer*	165
chapter eight	*It Happens*	181
	Acknowledgements	215

Introduction

Love, love, love. All you need is love. Let me count the ways. Certainly when couples marry, we generally think they are "in love." But how did they get there? What caused them to meet? How did they know this was THE person?

This book lets the reader in on stories of how people met their spouses. It does not pretend to be a scientific study offering a recipe to those looking for a partner or describing how to find "the one." Rather, this is a book to delight, entertain, and inspire you by reading the interesting, touching and unbelievable stories that people have shared. It may leave you in a state of awe at the variety of ways that people have met their partners. And, it may even help and inspire you in your own attempts to meet that special someone.

I have been asked many times how I thought of the idea of collecting stories of people meeting and marrying. I have had this idea for a long time. I know that women always want to know how a friend, sister, brother, whomever met the person they are dating. A number of men gave me their stories and I think they are interested, also.

I remember when I saw the movie, "When Harry Met Sally," I was caught up in the vignettes that were interspersed throughout the movie. The vignettes had older couples talking about their experiences of how they met their spouse. Everyone in the audience laughed at the innocence and uniqueness of the couples. This was further motivation for me to write this book and include those types of stories.

I began collecting the stories by first asking my closest circle of friends to share their stories. Once they all responded, I knew I was on my way. I realized early on that those who had been through divorce might not enjoy sharing their experience. Those who were able to and wanted to share were urged to participate.

There are many different types of stories, just as there are many different types of people. Some meetings were deliberate. Other introductions are quite out of the ordinary and unexpected. The difference in the older generation's meetings and those of the younger generation are marked. Are there differences among the practices of people from the U.S. and those people from other countries? Yes, there are and the stories bring out some of those differences in dating, courtship and marriage. In the end, however, girl meets boy and marriage is the result.

Every State in the U.S. is represented in the book as are a number of countries. People from all over loved having an outlet to tell their "juicy" stories. People thanked me for giving them the opportunity to "relive" the experience.

Please read them with attention to the ages of the couple and the year of the marriage since, in some cases, these facts make the story. Please note that the stories written in other than the first person are in most cases due to the couples having passed away. Some of the names and facts in the story have been changed at the request of the couple.

Ann and Sam Schneider
Dedication

Throughout my work on this project, I often thought of my own parents and how they met. I would have loved to begin the series of stories with my mother and father's story. Unfortunately my father died when my twin sister and I were babies. Even though I would ask my mother over the years how she met my father, she would never share the details with me. I am not sure whether it was for emotional reasons or not. She would just say that they met since they shared the same group of friends. She said that my father would "court" her by coming to her house and sitting in the "parlor" with her brother there as chaperon.

My parents were of different religions and, as you will see in some of the stories, the role of religion often plays a large part in people's lives. My mother didn't meet her in-laws until after she married my father. But the fact that I do not know exactly how my mother and father met is secondary to the wonderful connection that they shared. My mother and father were each born on Valentine's Day, February 14, of the same year. Despite religious issues they knew they were meant for each other. This book is dedicated to them and their loving relationship.

My mother passed away in June 2005. I started collecting my stories the following week with the feeling that she was by my side. I am sure she arranged for the good weather I experienced in all my travels and I feel that she guided me to meet wonderful people, without whose assistance I would never have completed this project.

Each of these stories in this book needs to be cherished since they are priceless to those who own them. In every case, they are unforgettable. I hope that you will find them the same.

Susan Schneider

Unforgettable
Vignettes of Love

chapter one

Persistence Pays Off

Mara and Patrick

as told by Mara.
Married in 1989 in Ocean Springs, Mississippi.
She was 25; he was 33.

Lose Some, Win Some

I was a news anchor for the local TV station and was assigned to cover a charity fundraiser. The event I was to cover was a bachelor auction. Women were to bid on available men and the money would go to the charity.

When I arrived at the auction, a few bachelors I already knew begged me to "purchase" them, even offering their credit cards to seal the deal. But it wasn't because they were dying to go out with me—it was because they were mortally afraid that no one would bid on them! I refused, because I believed their fears were unfounded and that it also wouldn't be appropriate for me to be bidding, when I was covering a news event.

However, when I saw Patrick, looking very tall, dark and handsome in his tux, my good intentions went mostly out the window. I attempted to bid on him surreptitiously, so the other bachelors would not find out, and it worked for a while. But when the bidding became more intense, I couldn't successfully conceal my attempts and was outbid.

Shortly after that event, I ran into Patrick. He recognized me from TV and we briefly flirted with each other. A few days later I was conducting man-on-the-street interviews on a controversial topic. He walked by and I pushed the microphone in his face to get his comments. We still didn't connect. "What does it take for this guy?" I remember thinking to myself.

Finally, I was invited to a cast party that the local theater was having. Patrick was there since he was the art director. Now we took the opportunity to flirt and chat and get to know each other better. I followed up by asking if he would like to go to a BB King concert with me. He responded with, "Wow!" We went and had a great time and were inseparable thereafter.

The following year, the Muscular Dystrophy Association decided to host the bachelor auction fundraiser again, and this time they called me to ask me to emcee the event! I was only too happy, as I was now engaged to the man who had first caught my eye at the same event the prior year. And when I arrived that evening and told one of the organizers my story, imagine my surprise when she informed me that she had met her husband of three years the same way.

Bethany and Michael

as told by Bethany.
Married in 2004 in Pensacola Beach, Florida.
She was 30; He was 34.

The Good Samaritan

I met Michael in the summer of 2001. My car tire went flat right on Buford Highway in Atlanta. I thought I would figure out what to do myself even though I had never changed a tire before. I was in the process of taking everything out of the trunk when this guy pulled over and asked me if I needed help. It was Michael. He started taking everything out of my trunk to get to the good tire. It was summer in Atlanta and incredibly hot. He was sweating but started to ask me questions, trying to make small talk. I thought it was strange that he was stopping to talk with me instead of just getting the job done—as it was so hot and he was sweating—but I felt comfortable talking with him. When he finished I offered to take him to lunch and he gave me his business card. After a few days when I went to look for the card, I realized I had lost it! I felt really badly as I had no way to get in contact with him. To my amazement, I found his card two months later! I remembered the promise that I made to take him to lunch and I also remembered that I felt comfortable with him. I called him and said, "Hey, this is tire girl. I owe you lunch if you are still interested." He said he was and we arranged to meet one afternoon the following week.

We had a normal "business" lunch for about one hour. I asked if he was dating anyone and he said no. He asked me the same question and I let him know that I was dating someone, but it was nothing serious. I was just asking to make conversation and not really thinking of dating him. The whole event was very nonchalant. We then went our separate ways.

After about one month Michael called me and asked how my tire was doing! He also asked how the "other" guy was doing. He would tell his friends that he considered me a "Tier 1 woman" and wanted to date me. He started to call me about once a month. I told my friends about him and they nicknamed him "Tire guy." In about the third month of his calling, I informed him that I was no longer dating the other guy. We agreed to go for dinner and we started dating. After one year we were engaged and married a year later. At the wedding we gave away tire gauges as part of the guest gifts.

Natasha and Konstantin

as told by Natasha.
Married in 1997 in Novosibirsk, Russia.
They were both 29.

Love Knows No Bounds

We met when we were 15 years old. We attended the same class in a physics-mathematical government high school for two years before going on to the university. There were 300 high school students from Central and Far East Russia and Siberia. Each of us was considered a top scholar in our hometown school and was handpicked to attend this school. I was one of 30 students in the class and there were only six girls. Since we all lived in the school dormitory we would see each other all day—in classes and after. Very soon Konstantin and I started spending a lot of time together but after a year, we broke up. It seemed to me at that time Konstantin wasn't as mature as I expected for a guy. From there our lives went in different ways and with different people.

Each of us married during our university years. My marriage didn't work out and after 8 years I divorced.

The class reunion from our school was coming up and I planned on going. When I arrived I noticed almost everyone from our class was there—Konstantin also. We all exchanged our business cards and talked about how everyone was doing. After a couple of hours of chatting I learned that in the 10 years since we graduated, Konstantin had married and had two children. However, he came alone and when we saw each other we realized that we still had feelings for each other. I saw him as more mature and more decisive in what he wanted in life. We danced, we talked—we couldn't get enough of each other. So many things happened, and so many words were said.

We spent that night together. Neither of us thought about the consequences; no one thought there would be any. But it was too great to forget about what happened. He called me and tried to see me a number of times and came by my house. At times, I did see him, although I told him I wanted more out of a relationship. It was a struggle for both of us. A few times we tried to break up. I dated other guys. He tried to reunite with his family but we always ended up together. It was tortuous! This communication went on for one and one half years. Konstantin didn't want to leave his children, but wanted to be with me. His wife knew Konstantin was not fully present in their marriage and one day she had enough and told him to leave. He showed up at my door with two suitcases. We lived together for three years before we finally married.

Sylvia and Albert

*as told by their daughter, Gail.
Married in 1934 in St. Louis, Missouri.
They were both 20. Albert died in 1999.*

The Way It Was

My mother and father were first married in 1934. They met two years earlier when my father frequented the general store that my mother's family owned, and she worked in. Dad saw my mother and thought, "what a beautiful young woman." From that moment on he was determined to meet her, to date her, and, if all went well, to hopefully win her over.

My mother played hard to get from the beginning. She was hesitant to give Dad any real attention on a personal basis, so he assumed the role of customer on his first visit, purchasing some small items and trying to make conversation. My mother felt that she had familial responsibilities and didn't think she should entertain male attention directed at her while working.

Undeterred, Dad continued to buy items from the store on several occasions, and mother continued to refrain from giving him the time of day.

My father thought my mother was smart and beautiful and he just plain liked her unique ways. He did everything he could to impress her, and my mother said in her own words that he was "smooth" and charming and she was initially afraid to trust his intentions.

Finally mother couldn't keep resisting his advances and invitations to go out with him. She finally said "okay" and agreed to join a group of his friends for a social event.

After a few casual dates, Mom learned from some relatives that Dad's family came from a town not far from the village in Russia where Mom was born. She was told that Dad's grandfather was learned in Jewish tradition and that his readings were "like pearls." The implication was that Dad came from a family with good stock.

The news of this high standing family reputation eased my mom's initial reticence and she dated Dad continually from that time. She still tried to "take the romance slowly and not rush into anything."

When my father popped the marriage question, my mother said she was scared to death. She needed him to go through the established protocol by asking her family for permission. However, he knew he didn't have the kind of job her parents would expect him to have and he didn't want to wait and allow others to interfere with his plans. He began pressing Mom to marry him and tell both sets of parents afterwards. Eventually mom submitted to the pressure and they eloped one evening across the state line and were married in secret by a justice of the peace.

On their wedding night she sat on the edge of the bed crying. She knew her parents would likely be very upset with her for eloping and for not having a traditional ceremony in the synagogue.

Right then and there she laid down the law to my father saying they would have to wait six months to begin married life together until they could have a religious wedding with the family's blessing. Dad conceded since he knew she was serious and he loved her so much. None of us children ever knew if the marriage was consummated that night or not.

Evie and Roland

as told by Evie.
Married in 1967 in Vienna, Austria.
She was 20; he was 21. They divorced in 1973.

Love Can Cure Heartbreak

We first met when I was 14 years old in Vienna. I was attending an all-girls school. The girls from the school would get together with a nearby boys' school to ensure our social skills were developed. Roland somehow came to one of these events even though he was not attending the boy's school.

All of the girls from my school thought Roland was very attractive, as did I. Over the next two years the attraction didn't wane since the girls in my school would see him at outside parties and then return to school and tell us about him. I was never in the "in" crowd at school and wore heavy eye makeup with my long red hair. However, one day I was invited to one of my classmate's houses for a party after a school event. Roland was at the party. All of the girls were very attentive to him. I never felt that I measured up to what he would want so I didn't engage in conversation with him. Oddly enough, he became interested in me and managed to get my phone number from someone. He called and asked me out but I didn't want to go. He was persistent in his calling and asking me out.

I had a boyfriend during this time and I became pregnant.

I decided with my parents not to keep the child and had an abortion. It was not legal at the time and I suffered through this painful and traumatic situation—forced to have the abortion on our kitchen table. My boyfriend was not supportive at all and I was beside myself with all that had transpired. But Roland was supportive, as I told him what I went through. He was caring and sympathetic to me. I looked at him in a new light and we started dating. Many women were jealous. We dated for three years and then married.

Donna and John

as told by Donna.
Married in 1992 in Foster, Rhode Island.
She was 41; he was 47.

Earning Trust

I was divorced and carrying on with my life and very involved in caring for my three children. It was summer and I would often go to an old swimming hole with a girlfriend of mine to cool off from the summer heat and meet other friends. There were a number of people who would stop by the area since it was in a park and was a nice, relaxing place to be.

One day a man drove up and came over to the swimming hole. He started talking to the group of people we were with. I didn't pay him much attention but soon he was talking with me. His name was John. The next time he showed up he asked me if I wanted to go for a ride on his motorcycle. I agreed and found that I enjoyed talking with him. He asked me if I wanted to kiss him and I said I didn't think so. We had never met before even though he lived down the street from me.

We continued to see each other with our friends but I was very reluctant to start a relationship. I enjoyed being with him but I also wanted to care for my children. So, when he asked me out on a date we went to McDonald's with my children, too. We then went back to my house and watched a movie.

    We continued dating but I was too afraid to trust him. He had never been married and was 40 years old—I thought there must have been something wrong. It wasn't until I met his mother and brother did I start to trust him. He was very patient with me and knew that I wanted to raise my children before I would be serious with anyone. We dated for seven years. By then my children were grown and had moved on with their lives. John and I decided to build a house together. Once the house was completed we moved in and married soon after.

Michelle and Pete

as told by Michelle.
Married in 1993 in Pensacola, Florida.
She was 23; he was 24.

With A Little Help from My Friend

I was married at 19 to my high school sweetheart. He was in the military and was stationed in Wichita, Kansas. Being a southern girl and not used to the cold weather, Kansas was certainly different than anything I had experienced. I knew where Kansas was on the map but certainly had never been there, nor had I a desire to go.

Once we settled in Kansas, I began working in a bank. The same day I began my training at the bank, so did a guy named Pete who had just graduated from college in Lawrence, Kansas. The training videos were rather boring so we talked about things in our own life:

families and other general things. I felt like he had always been in my life since we were just so at ease and comfortable with each other, not to mention how cute I thought he was.

Pete told me he felt like he had met the woman of his dreams but she was taken. In the meantime, my marriage was falling apart. I figured the fact that my husband and I had been so young when we married and were not really sharing the same goals or ambitions in life was bound to lead to problems. Plus, the military life didn't help as he stayed out later and later drinking and hanging around his buddies.

I went to work everyday and became very close friends with Pete and a girl named Kelli. We all went out to dinner and the movies and had a good time.

My husband moved out and basically said he didn't want to be married anymore. Kelli and I moved in together. Pete desperately wanted to ask me out but didn't know if the timing was right and certainly didn't know how I felt. He felt as though he had loved me since the day he met me. Kelli told Pete to plan a weekend for all three of us to visit Lawrence, Kansas where he went to college. Pete coordinated it and we all were set to go when Kelli backed out at the last minute. Pete and I went anyway, not yet knowing that this was a plan devised by her for us to be alone.

During out trip, several songs kept playing on the radio that seemed fitting—the songs were about loving someone. We ended up having a wonderful weekend. Pete showed me around the campus and we had lunch at his favorite sub shop. I met his friends that were still there at college. That first day he bought me a sweatshirt with the university logo on it. He handed it to me to as he kissed me for the first time. He told me he had wanted to do that since the moment he met me while watching training videos at the bank. We took it slow, dating for a while, both scared that I was just rebounding. Eventually, I took him to Pensacola to meet my family and they all loved him. Secretly they never wanted the first marriage to take place, anyway.

That Christmas, Pete proposed. He had already told my parents and showed them the ring. We were married the next spring. Pete wanted to go to law school and I wanted to be out of Kansas. We ended up in Alabama.

If it weren't for the first marriage of two young people who weren't soul mates, then Pete and I would have certainly never met. I would never have been in Kansas and I doubt a Kansas boy would have been in the South. Sometimes, you have to go through the wrong or bad to find what you are meant to have. Certainly life throws curveballs at you, but I think we managed to catch them or dodge our way around them.

Lori and Kevin

as told by Lori.
Married in 1992 in Hopkinton, New Hampshire.
They were both 27.

10

Even though I was attending the same college as Kevin and living in the same townhouse complex, we had not met. We were both seniors at Ithaca College in 1987. Kevin knew who I was since he and his friends spied on my roommates and me while we were sunbathing by viewing us through their telephoto lenses. Kevin gave me the nickname "10." He wanted to introduce himself and left me a note on my car one day saying hello and signing it, "the guy in the Jeep." Since I didn't recall seeing anyone driving around in a Jeep, I let it go.

Interestingly, we knew many of the same people. Kevin would see me on different occasions when he was with his friends playing in the local band. We had a mutual friend named Randy who worked for the band and belonged to the same ski club as I did. Randy knew that my nickname was "10." One night Randy was at the same bar as me and Kevin's band was playing. Randy was standing with me and he pointed to Kevin and said, "See that guy up at the drums? I shouldn't tell you this, but he's in love with you. And he is the nicest person you will ever meet." At break time, Randy introduced me to Kevin. We talked and had a drink. On another occasion, I went to listen to the band with one of my friends. That was the night Kevin sang and played the drums. I was so impressed.

We met up later at a friend's house. A group of us went swimming in the gorges, of which there are plenty in Ithaca. When we returned to the house, Kevin and I stayed up all night talking. Now Kevin was asking me out on a regular basis. However, graduation took place and I was going on to Vermont to start my career. Kevin was staying in Ithaca to continue with the band. I was so sad to leave. Kevin knew it and gave me a dozen roses to see me off. Thus began our five years of commuting to see each other on weekends within Vermont, Vermont to New Hampshire, New Hampshire to Connecticut, etc., depending on where each one of us decided to work.

At one point Kevin worked for an organization that had a policy that if you gave blood, you could leave early on Friday. He would give blood often just to be able to leave early to see me! He racked up a number of speeding tickets, too.

The commuting continued and Kevin still played in a band as a starving performer. He felt he didn't have the money for an engagement ring and marriage so he delayed proposing. One weekend I was driving to Connecticut to see Kevin, and I found myself stuck in a bad snowstorm and had to stay the night in a hotel. The next day my car hit a pothole. By the time I arrived at Kevin's, I'd had it with the commute and the number of years of waiting. I told my family that I wanted to break off the relationship but my family was furious with me since they loved Kevin. I couldn't break up with him. That spring, he finally proposed and we married the next fall.

Brittni and Michael

as told by Brittni.
Married in 2003 in Aberdeen, South Dakota.
They were both 22.

Crazy in Love

I was dating a guy from my hometown for five years when I moved to Aberdeen to attend college. My roommate Courtney was working at a local restaurant and invited me to go there with her one day to see where she worked. When we came into the restaurant area I spotted a guy she worked with. I said to Courtney, "If I didn't have this boyfriend, I would go after that guy." It was Michael. Courtney introduced us and I must have shown more interest than I thought as he mentioned later that I was "overwhelming."

During this time, Michael contracted cancer. He was at work infrequently since he had to go for treatment several times a week. I was now employed at the same restaurant and was able to see him on those occasions when he worked. I was still crazy about him and was now free to overwhelm him even more since my long-term boyfriend broke off our relationship. Once our friends turned 21, we went out often as a group. Michael was one of them. He was back at work and Courtney was filling his ears all the time telling him how interested I was in him.

By this point he was showing interest in me when we were

with the group by being affectionate and kissing me. However, he basically ignored me when we were at work. I was so confused. I wondered if I should stick with this guy who was undergoing this serious physical condition. In short time, another guy who I met became interested in me and I decided to accept his requests to date. Michael now suspected that I was not as interested in him and asked me if there was someone else. I told him there was and he immediately wanted to spend more time with me.

That was the key to my getting Michael. We were engaged three months later and married the next year.

Jackie and Joe

as told by Joe.
Married in 1960 in Lebanon, Tennessee.
She was 18; he was 19.

Seizing The Moment

We were raised in Lebanon, Tennessee, a small rural community 30 miles east of Nashville. It is possible that I have known Jackie since she was in her bassinet. Our parents grew up in Lebanon and had known each other during their high school years. They were friends and were raising their families at the same time. When we were young, our families vacationed together several times in the summers. So it is true that we have virtually known each other all of our lives.

Jackie was a very pretty girl. As I became of dating age, it was only natural that I should have some interest in her. However, that was complicated by the fact that she was dating my best friend, Don. We had even double-dated a few times.

Jackie's grandfather owned a small restaurant in Lebanon called the Orange Bar where Jackie worked on Saturdays. Whenever possible, I had lunch there when she worked, always sitting at the counter where she served customers. One Saturday in August I was having lunch at the Orange Bar and whenever she had a moment we would talk. I knew that she'd had a date with Don the previous evening. She informed me that they decided to break up. I must confess that I was not deeply disappointed by the news. I seized the moment and, with some anxiety, asked her out for that evening. To my great joy, she accepted. At the time, I was a sophomore in high school and she was a freshman.

Lebanon had a drive-in movie theater, which ran first-run movies. I took her to the drive-in and did my best to impress her so that she would be interested in a future date. The date seemed to start well, but appeared to take a bad turn when she fell into a deep sleep midway through the movie, only for her to awaken when we were leaving to return to her house. I was greatly concerned, as the evening's events didn't portend a great future romance.

We had a second date two weeks later and I was heartened by the fact that she stayed awake through the entire movie! We dated throughout high school. We became engaged in January of Jackie's senior year and married in December of that year.

Janice and Mike

as told by Janice.
Married in 1975 in Milwaukee, Wisconsin.
She was 18; he was 19. They divorced in 1985.

Big Brother Is Watching!

I met Mike when we were in the same class in high school in Milwaukee. I was one of 13 children and had eight brothers. Mike came from a family of seven children, three girls and four boys. I would talk with Mike in class and I knew that Mike was interested in me. Mike would try to get my girlfriends to go by my house late at night and get me to come out so Mike could see me. My brother, who was closest to me in age, found out that Mike wanted to date me. This one brother was very protective of me. My brother told Mike to leave me alone, as I was too young to date. Mike and I continued our friendship and when I turned 16 my brother gave me permission to date Mike.

Once I turned 18 and things began to look serious enough for marriage, my mother became involved and decided that she didn't want her daughter to marry Mike and sent me to Seattle to join my older brother who lived there. I was very upset, as I wanted to marry Mike. Mike wanted to marry me and decided he would join the service and get stationed in Seattle, which he did. Once both of us were living in Seattle it became inevitable that we would marry.

My family realized that there was nothing they could do so they reluctantly agreed to a wedding. The wedding was held back in Milwaukee with both of our large families attending.

The marriage lasted 10 years and produced a daughter and two sons. To this day Mike and I are best friends! Mike's family still thinks highly of me and still calls me their sister-in-law.

Jenna and Tony

as told by Tony.
Married in 2004 in Old Greenwich, Connecticut.
She was 30; he was 38.

I'm In Trouble!

I had bumped into Jenna several times since her sister-in-law's parents were good friends with my parents. I thought she was cute. However, I didn't want to meet anyone and get serious since I was in a social coma after my divorce. I wanted to be single the rest of my life. I knew that Jenna was dating someone, but her family was disappointed that the relationship continued for so long without any long-term commitment.

At a New Year's Eve party, I had a chance to talk with her more. Her brother organized a dance contest as part of the night's fun and Jenna won. We had danced most of the evening together even though she was there with her boyfriend. I had said to her, "When is this 'ja-moke' going to ask you to marry him?" I said, "If you are not married by age 35, what do you say we get hitched?" She was not sure that I was really interested in her since I was older and she thought I may have been thinking of her as "the little sister." At this point though, she was showing some interest by casually questioning her brother about me.

I had been in her company on another occasion when she was with her brother and a group of friends at their house. The friends put a fart machine under her chair without her knowing. When they let it go she acted as if she really had farted and excused herself. I thought she was cool the way she handled that. She seemed to be a lot of fun.

Then it was Easter Sunday and our families were all together for dinner. I knew that Jenna had recently broken off with her boyfriend, but I pretended as if it was news to me. I asked her if she wanted to go to lunch with me sometime. I asked her for her business card but she didn't give it to me. She claimed in later conversations that she was afraid that I was playing with her and she was confused not knowing if I really was interested in her. She thought it all seemed too perfect to work out. In addition she wanted to play the social scene in NYC where she was living since breaking off her last relationship.

However, I continued pursuing her since I now felt tired of meeting women who meant nothing to me. I was able to get her number from her sister-in-law and called her when I was in NYC for the day. I asked her to dinner and she accepted. I saw her walking down the street to meet me after her work that day and I thought she looked cute. I told myself, "I am in trouble." We had a great time together. Afterwards I walked her to the door and tried to kiss her but missed! So I went for another and this time I made sure that I gave her a memorable kiss. I was jazzed after meeting her. As I was driving home I was listening to the radio, which was playing all love songs. I sang all the way home! She confessed later on to daydreaming about her wedding for the first time in her life after our date.

The next time I saw her, I presented her with a bottle of ketchup instead of flowers because I knew she loved ketchup. She fell for me after that.

We continued dating and had a lot of laughs. I gave her a trip to go skydiving with me, which we were looking forward to very much. I planned to present her with an engagement ring and propose during the dive, but I realized that I couldn't take the box with the ring in it on the dive since it might fall out. So I mouthed the words while we were being videotaped during the dive and showed the video to her afterwards. She couldn't figure out what I was saying! Later that evening, I took her out on the balcony of our hotel overlooking the ocean and popped the question. To my relief, she accepted. We went to a restaurant that evening to celebrate and enjoy our excitement. On the way out, I was yelling to everyone there, "I'm going to marry this woman." We were married six months later.

chapter two

Love at First Sight

Tina and Tim

as told by Tina.
Married in 1994 in Milford, Delaware.
She was 24; he was 25.

Sir, I Do, Sir!

I was working at the Delaware State Police Training Academy in a part-time clerical position. I went to the cafeteria for lunch as I did each day with a coworker. The recruits from the current class were lined up against the wall military style waiting to go to lunch since they respectfully let the office staff ahead of them. All of those recruits looked good to me since I was in an off-again-on-again relationship at the time. However, people at the Academy had tried to set me up twice before with recruits from previous classes and it hadn't worked out.

I was standing at the end of the long lunch line and I was noticeably sticking out of the cafeteria so it was possible that the recruits could see me. The drill instructor caught one of the guys named Tim looking at me instead of staring straight ahead and said in his authoritative voice, "Shockley, are you looking at that girl?"

Tim answered, "Sir, yes sir."

"Do you think that girl is pretty, Shockley?"

"Sir, yes sir."

"Shockley, would you like to go out with that girl?"

"Sir, I would not mind, sir."

That must not be what he should have said. The drill instructor said, "Drop and give me 20!" Poor Tim. He had to do 20 pushups right there.

What Tim didn't know is that the drill instructor knew my family and me. He also didn't know that the drill instructor had already pointed Tim's picture out to me from the gallery of pictures of recruits on a wall in the Academy. He said that he thought Tim had his head on straight and would be good for me. I was not interested in meeting any of them and didn't associate the Tim in the picture with the Tim in the line by the cafeteria.

At the end of the training, there was always a party for the recruits. I was invited to go by one of my coworkers but felt that the guys would all be playing pool and doing "guy" things, so I wasn't too interested. This same evening I had an argument with my on-again, off-again boyfriend. I was home crying and my coworker called and told me that Tim wanted to meet me and persuaded me to come to the party. I said, "Okay, I'm coming!" I went and spent the night getting to know Tim. When I went home that night I told myself that I was going to marry him.

By recruit graduation, I had already checked Tim out by

reviewing his personnel records, which I had access to, including his psychological evaluation! I had also heard that he had a relationship with an on-again, off-again girlfriend. She came to Tim's graduation but he suggested she leave since he wanted to be with me. I worked at the graduation and met up with Tim at the reception following the ceremony. We exchanged phone numbers and he said he would call me. I anxiously waited for him to call. After a week, I called him. He was very surprised to hear from me. We talked on the phone and then he found the nerve to ask me out. I, of course, accepted.

    I had always envisioned the guy that I wanted to marry. Tim was that guy. We dated for almost two years before we were engaged. We married two years later after I earned my bachelors degree and Tim became a state trooper.

Tillie and Pete

as told by Tillie to her niece, Louise.
Married in 1935 in Portland, Oregon.
She was 22; he was 23. Tillie died in 2006; Pete died in 1998.

Keeping It In The Family:
Three Brides for Three Brothers

Tillie was a member of the Sacred Heart Church choir. On selected Sundays, Mass was offered for the men in the parish and their sons. Tillie happened to look down from the choir loft and saw a guy with a beautiful head of hair who was in the procession of men entering the church. It was Pete and he had come to church with his father and brothers. Immediately, after seeing him she knew she wanted to find a way to get to know him. She planned to wait until after Mass and be at the doorway of the church when the congregation was departing and "accidentally" drop her open purse. Being the gentleman she assumed he would be he would help her gather her things. Well, unfortunately, this never came to pass because choir members were required to stay and sing another song at the dismissal and she missed him. She was heartsick.

A short time later she accepted an invitation to a birthday party at a friend's house. When she arrived she saw many people milling about and soon noticed the same man at the party whom she noticed at church. She discovered it was her friend's brother,

Pete. Someone at the party introduced Tillie to Pete and she knew right then that they were meant to be. They talked together for a long time at the party and Pete asked if he could drive her home. She readily accepted. In her telling of the story she said "of course" she accepted, with a devilish little smile on her face since she "fell flat" for Pete when she saw him. No kisses were exchanged as that was not proper on a first date but after that the two became inseparable. They were married in Sacred Heart Church.

Florence (Flea) and Joseph

as told by Tillie to her niece, Louise.
Married in 1939 in Portland, Oregon.
She was 22; he was 25. Florence died in 1999; Joseph died in 1990.

Tillie came from a family of ten children and Pete came from a family of six. Both Tillie and Pete had chosen a brother and sister to stand up for them at their wedding. Tillie asked Flea and Pete asked his brother Joe. Both Flea and Joe were dating others at the time but as soon as they met they were one. They dated and fell in love and also married at Sacred Heart Church.

Patricia and Chris

as told by Tillie to her niece, Louise.
Married in 1946 in Portland, Oregon.
She was 27; he was 26. Patricia died in 1999; Chris died in 1994.

When it was time for Flea and Joe's wedding, each chose a brother and sister to stand up for them. Joe asked his brother Chris, and Flea asked her sister Pat. They had been much younger when

Tillie and Pete married and coming from such large families, they had not met each other before. Pat and Chris started dating and Chris went off to World War II. When he returned from the war, they got married too! It was now officially, three brides for three brothers.

Of course, the children from these three couples all had the same set of grandparents and growing up they thought it strange when they would come upon a cousin from the other aunts and uncles who had different grandparents!

Nevenka and Joseph

as told by Nevenka.
Married in 1962 in Sarajevo, Bosnia and Herzegovina.
She was 32; he was 57. Joseph died in 1967.

Those Shoes!

It was love at first sight. It happened on a ship while the ship was docked in Split-Hvar in Croatia, in the summer of 1961. There was a great mood on the ship since everyone was having fun looking at the dolphins in the water. I was with my mother and we were sitting on the deck of the ship. I was looking down when I suddenly saw this elegant pair of shoes in front of me. I raised my eyes and the gentleman wearing the shoes smiled at me.

We talked and I explained that I came from Sarajevo. He told me his name was Joseph and bet me that I wasn't born yet when he was in the army in Sarajevo. Before we left the ship to spend our vacation on the island of Hvar, we arranged to meet the next morning. We did meet the next morning and every morning thereafter for walks on the beach. We married shortly after and spent six years together before Joseph passed away. We had one child together and I never remarried.

Patricia and Albert

as told by Albert.
Married in 1974 in San Diego, California.
She was 32; he was 37.

The Favor

I had a college buddy, Phil, whom I maintained a friendship with. Phil was married to Robin and they lived across the street from a woman named Pat. Phil thought I would be interested in Pat even though Pat and I were each dating other people casually. Robin asked Pat if she would be interested in going on a blind date. Pat thought she owed the neighbors a favor so she agreed to go on the blind date with me on Friday, 13th of September 1974.

Upon meeting, both Pat and I felt it was love at first sight. I called her the next day to go out. However, I could not get a hold of her and found out through others that she was in the hospital getting her tubes tied. She had made the appointment before we ever met and was probably more convinced to go ahead with the operation when she found out that I had five children from my previous marriage. After a few days I was able to reach her when she was home from the hospital. We went out on a second date and then continued to see each other almost every day. On the eighth day after meeting each other, I proposed to Pat and she readily accepted. She was working as a flight attendant and had to go on a trip. When she returned, she told me that she still loved me but wanted to be sure of one thing—she didn't want any children! I knew I had found my match and said to her, "Thank God!" We now have 36 grandchildren to date from my five children. I know that Pat was a gift from God.

Jill and Mike

as told by Jill.
Married in 1994 in Morro Bay, California.
They were both 35.

High School Reunion

We actually met in Mt. Whitney High School in Visalia, California. I think we probably met when Mike was in the high school band. He played the saxophone. I was a "letter girl," meaning I had no other responsibility than to carry the letter "E" in the front of the band when they marched into the football stadium. I don't recall much more about Mike in high school other than that.

Many years later when we were both 34 years old, we met again around Christmas time. We were both single and had completed our many years of higher education and had careers. But when you are single and in your 30's, you still "go home" to your mom and dad's house for Christmas. During the holidays, both of us happened to be in Visalia at a mutual friend's house for a little wine and cheese gathering. We talked at the party and really hit it off. We remembered that we had not seen each other since graduation, 16 years ago. We recapped much of what had transpired for each of us in those intervening years.

At the end of the gathering, I was supposed to catch a ride with my girlfriend but since I wanted to hang around at the party awhile, Mike, with a big smile on his face, offered to give me a ride to my folks' house at the end of the night. On the way home, he asked if I was busy and could I go grab a bite to eat for dinner. I said, sure, I was available. He took me to the nicest restaurant in town. What he didn't know yet was that I was scheduled to meet up with some friends but I decided to stand them up for a chance to go out with Mike.

Unfortunately, I was "caught" in my own lie because when we entered the restaurant, my friends also came to the very same restaurant and saw me with Mike! Fortunately, they knew immediately what was going on and gave me a wry smile. We had a lovely evening, and then he came to my home for dinner the very next night. We knew very soon after that we were the right match for each other. We became officially engaged the following October, and were married in April.

One joke we still toss around is that Mike remembers actually having a date with me in high school, but I don't remember it!

Lori and Mark

as told by Lori.
Married in 1986 in Louisville, Kentucky.
She was 24; he was 27.

The Dedicated Doctor

Mark was a first-year resident in a hospital and I was working nights as a nurse on the neurosurgery floor. Residents in surgery rotate specialties every month. In November, Mark went up to my floor to check it out since he was starting there in December. He told a number of the nurses that he didn't know anything about neurosurgery and didn't want to know. He just wanted to get through the month. Mark and I were introduced when he started on the floor. We both thought the other person was attractive. The other nurses told me not to go out with him as they thought of him as a "player." We started flirting with each other and Mark asked me out by the end of December. We were engaged six months later.

Mark received the Neurosurgery Rotator of the Year award in June. The administration thought that he was so dedicated to neurosurgery when he was actually coming up to see me all the time! We were married about one and a half years from the time we started dating. I feel that it has been marital bliss ever since.

Claire and Kevin

as told by Claire.
Married in 1989 in Iowa City, Iowa.
She was 23; he was 26.

Daddy's Little Girl

I met my husband Kevin through my cousin. They were best friends in college. One day, walking through the campus I met up with the two of them. We were introduced and spoke briefly. Later that day I went back to my dorm and told my roommate that I had met the guy that I was going to marry! Months later my cousin's parents were having an anniversary party in Iowa. My cousin had invited Kevin and he flew in to attend the party. He didn't have a car, so I was asked to pick him up from the airport and take him to the party. We had a good time talking on the drive.

I had a nine-year relationship that was winding down. My long-time boyfriend didn't like to attend family events so he didn't accompany me to the party. Once at the party, Kevin and I danced and had a great time. I realized that I was so crazy in love with him that I could hardly breath while we were dancing. My face felt like it was on fire. My father saw us and decided that we were dancing too close. He interrupted our dance and asked me to dance with him instead. After the party we went our separate ways. Kevin was dating other women at the time and was happy to keep this dating pattern going.

I did keep an eye out for him on campus. Several times I rode my bicycle by the Engineering building where he attended classes. We did finally "run into" each other and agreed to meet at the Field House and play basketball. That was when we exchanged phone numbers.

Later that week he phoned and invited me to join him and a group of friends at one of his favorite bars. I loved his friends and we had great fun dancing together again. From then on we would chat on the telephone for long periods of time. Our apartments were about half a mile apart. During one conversation we decided to both leave our apartments and meet in the alley and see who could get there the quickest. From then on we were a couple and went on to marry.

Lucy and Gary

as told by Gary.
Married in 1979 in Minneapolis, Minnesota.
She was 28; he was 26.

When One Door Shuts, Another One Opens

I was studying for my vocal music degree in graduate school, in Texas. Lucy was attending Concordia College, in Minnesota. We were serving as apprentice artists for the Opera Company and were both selected to perform at the Colorado Opera Festival for the summer.

At the first day of staging rehearsal, we were both in a dance line. Lucy was to stand in front of me and I was to wrap my arms around her waist. The title of the opera that we were rehearsing for was "Elixir of Love." We got right into it. Our dancing was probably more romantic than was required of us but we both knew that we were attracted to each other. After rehearsal we all went for pizza. I invited Lucy back to my room as we were all staying in the same college dorm. Lucy was surprised at how fast we found each other but she agreed to come back to my room. A lot of kissing went on that night!

One problem—we were both dating other people. My girlfriend called and announced she was coming to visit me. She was staying at a nearby hotel. I had decided to break off with her. When I went to her room and told her, she threw an ashtray at me. It hit the door and so did I. Lucy had an easier time breaking off her relationship with her hippie boyfriend. We then continued to see each other.

Opening night was about six weeks after we met. We were at a party at a friend's house after the performance and dressed in our tuxes and formal gowns. I took hold of the celebratory moment to kneel down by the swimming pool and propose to Lucy in front of everyone. She accepted. After that our friends threw us both into the pool!

Once we finished with the Opera Company, I headed back to Texas and Lucy to Minnesota. I moved to Minnesota in November and we married a month later.

Pam and Angelo

as told by Pam.
Married in 1967 in Yonkers, New York.
She was 19; he was 24.

Checking Her Out!

It was the spring of 1965 when I was a junior in high school and starting my first part-time job at the local Grand Union Supermarket as a cashier. I was 17. Angelo had just been discharged from the United States Navy and was employed at the Grand Union as a senior grocery clerk. We were immediately attracted to each other when we met. We started getting to know each other through the normal chatter and flirting, which went on daily.

One day we were in the employees' lounge by ourselves and took advantage of the moment to share our first kiss! It wasn't long before Angelo was walking me home every night. Next, he was staying regularly for my family's delicious Italian dinners. Often Angelo would take the bus home to Mount Vernon where he lived with his mother and sister. He didn't own a car, which was not uncommon. Occasionally, my father would drive him home. We wondered if that was my father's way of getting to know this guy that their daughter was so taken with!

Soon, Angelo bought his first car—a used 1962 Oldsmobile convertible. Our relationship was moving forward and I met his family. We both had large families counting all the cousins, aunts and uncles. Most of our family customs were similar since our two families were of Italian descent.

By the spring of 1966, on my 18th birthday, we became engaged. An engagement party was planned but was soon cancelled when my dad had his first heart attack four days before the party was to happen. He recovered and life moved forward.

We married in the spring, 1967. It was a beautiful day!

Marjorie and Andrew

as told by Marjorie.
Married in 1946 in Wibaux, Montana.
She was 24; he was 25.

Never Too Shy

I arrived by train in Marmarth, North Dakota in September 1944 to teach at the local grade school. In November, the school sponsored a fund-raising carnival, which I attended with a male friend. Andrew attended the carnival with his date. My friend was a distant relative of Andrew's and so he introduced us. Andrew said it was "love at first sight."

A few days later Andrew wanted to ask me for a date. This was before anyone in Marmarth had telephones and he was also somewhat shy. He drove around town until he saw a friend. He wanted her to go to the boarding house where I lived to ask me to go bowling with him. The friend asked me on behalf of Andrew and I was thrilled! This was our first date.

We began seeing each other more often. Sometimes our date would be horseback riding at the ranch that Andrew helped his father operate. We continued dating, and I received a diamond and a marriage proposal at Christmas in 1945. We were married in St. Peter's Church in Wibaux, Montana, which was my hometown. We were married in a beautiful stone church, which is now on the register of historic places in Montana.

Ann Marie and Keith

as told by Keith.
Married in 1961 in Reno, Nevada.
They were both 22.

Why Wait?

Ann Marie was attending college in California. I was in the U.S. Air Force. One night I went with my buddies to a local pizza parlor that served German beer and had German bands. It was a big college student hangout. I was interested in meeting someone and found myself talking to a woman who was not all that interested in me. A few minutes later her cousin came over and we hit it off right away. Her name was Ann Marie. I asked her out and she accepted. We saw each other every day for the next week. At the end of the week, I proposed. Ann Marie responded by saying, "I wondered when you were going to ask me. What took you so long?"

The Air Force schedule caused us to continually change our plans to marry. We set a date for the wedding at a church in Reno, although I still had three months to go in my flight training. I was on duty the night before the wedding and didn't get off until 1:00 a.m. I then left for Reno with my service buddies, who were our best man and ushers. They insisted that we go to a floorshow at a casino since they hadn't given me a bachelor party. We finally left about 5:00 a.m. and collapsed for a few hours before the wedding ceremony!

Louise and Robert

as told by Louise.
Married in 1961 in Springvale, Maine.
She was 23; he was 25.

Better Late Than Never

A group of my friends were getting together and wanted me to meet one of their friends named Robert. I said yes, but after thinking about it, I really didn't want to go. Another one of my friends wanted to go to a club and wanted someone to go with. She convinced me that I didn't want to go on this date. She said it would be more fun for me to go with her to the club, so I went. I never said anything to any of my friends about standing Robert up and never called him.

After one year—one year, Robert contacted me! He was calling to ask me out. For reasons unknown now, I said yes to his request. We were to go out with the same group as the year before. He planned to stand *me* up but after he thought about it, he changed his mind since he knew if he did he would be alone like the last time. Instead we went out and had a great time. We both agreed it was love at first sight.

Robert and I had not discussed marriage yet but I told a friend of mine that I was going to marry him. My friend asked how I knew that when he had not even proposed to me. I told her he would, and he did on New Years Eve, in 1960, while we were on the dance floor. We dated another one and a half years before marrying.

Josephine and Louis

as told by Josephine.
Married in 1942 in Monsanto, Washington.
She was 21; he was 23.

Against Family Wishes

We met through relatives, as we were part of the same family. My uncle married Louis's aunt. We saw each other infrequently at family gatherings when we were younger. Now that we were dating age and met again at a cousin's party, we knew we were meant to be.

Louis asked me for a date later that night at the party, which I accepted. We both enjoyed being with each other and we started dating regularly. It was difficult for us to date because I lived in the Bronx where my mother and I moved to be with an aunt and uncle after my father passed away. Louis lived about one hour away in New Jersey. We would meet in Manhattan for our dates but my aunt and uncle said I had to be home by 10:00 p.m. Louis was quite the gentleman and he would take the subway almost to my stop to ensure my safety, even though travel was relatively safe compared to today. He then had to take a train in the opposite direction to get back to his home in New Jersey.

After he entered the service, he was stationed in Fort Dix, New Jersey. Soon after, the attack on Pearl Harbor happened.

The U.S. government believed that the Japanese might attack the west coast of the U.S. mainland. Louis was transferred to Fort Lewis, Washington, a long way from New Jersey for me. We communicated often by writing letters and talking on the phone whenever possible. After one year of that we decided to marry because we thought Louis would be transferred overseas. However, Louis could not get away from his service duties so the only way for us to marry was for me to travel to Washington.

I announced our decision to my mother. She was devastated that I was not going to have a big Italian wedding. I was young and insistent that our decision was what we wanted and I could only think of being with Louis. My uncle promised me the biggest wedding in the world if I waited and married later in New York. I would not change my mind.

I took a three-day trip by train to Fort Lewis, WA to be with Louis. When I arrived he met me at the train and we immediately drove to the justice of the peace to be married. We knew that our families would never forgive us if we lived with each other without being married. Louis started Officers Training School and I went back to the Bronx to live with my mother. After he graduated he was transferred to Louisiana and I met him there. Next he was transferred overseas and I moved back again to live with my mother. Finally, he returned from the service and we made our life together.

Betty and Doran

as told by Betty.
Married in 1957 in Casper, Wyoming.
She was 18; he was 20. Doran died in 1999.

A Million Dollar Baby

I first saw my future husband when he was working as a soda jerk at Walgreen's. I went in to the store with my mother and Doran began flirting with me. My mother was mad at him since she considered me too young to have someone flirting with me. The next time I saw him I was working at Woolworth's Five and Dime store. By then Doran worked in the dental lab next door and would come in and buy a candy bar from me every day. I knew he was for me from the time I first saw him. He stuck out and I was immediately attracted to him.

Finally, I saw him at the local skating rink. He wanted to meet me but never had the courage to introduce himself. So he had his cousin come up to me at the rink and tell me that he had someone he wanted me to meet. We met and started dating from that point on. We were engaged in a few months and married the following year. He told everyone from then on that he found his million-dollar baby in a Five and Ten Cent store!

Julie and Toby

as told by Toby.
Married in 2000 in Flagstaff, Arizona.
She was 26; he was 31.

Fantasy Girl

It was October 1995 and I was attending the local college in Flagstaff. It was homecoming week, which meant that it was Tequila Sunrise time. The bars are open at 6:00 a.m. and the streets are shut down with people playing pool, dancing, drinking and partying.

I was at a bar called The Depot with my friend Joel. We had been cruising and looking at chicks. When we arrived at The Depot, people were dancing. I noticed a girl wearing a blue Hawaiian-type skirt, with a slit down the side and a half-top on and long brown hair. My immediate response was "Wow!" She was a great dancer and I could not keep my eyes off of her. Talk about perfect abs and ooh, the way she moved! I just had to have her. It was the type of want that if I could not make her mine I would be depressed for weeks.

After two hours Joel was sick of my pointing out all her special talents and features to him. He told me that he was going to tell her that I wanted to dance with her. Shock began to set in since I cannot dance and was mortified that he was actually approaching her. I ran the other way toward another part of the bar and before I reached the other end I felt the delicate tap of a hand on my shoulder. When I turned around it was Julie—the woman I had been eyeing for hours! Instant jubilation and horror raced to my heart as she asked me if I wanted to dance. When I told her that I didn't know how, she offered to show me. I felt like a fool on the dance floor, but also knew that I wanted her badly enough to risk feeling foolish. We talked while dancing to several songs and I summoned the nerve to invite her to a party I was going to later that day. I also told her where I lived.

Soon, her wicked girlfriend showed up and dragged her away. Julie had a boyfriend in Phoenix and her friend felt obliged to keep her true to him by not having her meet anyone else. I could only pray that she showed at the party.

I went to the party and, although I normally would have been working to pick up a woman, I thought I would behave in case Julie showed. No way was I going to blow this chance. I played pool and looked at the door every 5 minutes, hoping she would show. She never did. I was so disappointed and felt like such a fool.

Two weeks later I was in my apartment and there was a knock on the door. I opened it to find Julie! She was in the neighborhood but could not stay. At this point I remember thinking, "Oh yeah, she wants me!"

We arranged to drive to the mountains a few days later to get together. After that date, we spoke on the phone a few times. Then we bumped into each other again at The Depot where we danced and had our first kiss. That was it for Julie. She dumped her boyfriend and we started dating. Since we were both nervous about getting married, we chose to live together for four years. Then one day I came home from work and said, "Let's go to town, we're getting married." So we went to the justice of the peace and married.

chapter three

Ups and Downs and Ups

Kathy and Jerry

as told by Jerry.
Married in 1973 in Innerkip, Ontario, Canada.
She was 27; he was 21.

Opposites Attract!

Meeting my wife Kathy saved my life.

Kathy was born, raised and educated in England before finishing her education degree at a university in Michigan. While she was in Michigan she became involved in spiritual renewal. She applied to a Canadian church school to teach and was hired for a job in Paris, Ontario. One Sunday she visited the local Christian drop-in center to learn more about it for her students. She knocked on the door and I answered. I was tall and hippy-looking, with long blond hair; a look, which I found out later, was not attractive to her.

I thought she was very cute and had a shapely figure. She asked a lot of questions about the center so I suggested she come back in a few hours when my brother, who ran the center, would be there.

Kathy did return and even started attending Bible study classes at the center in addition to services at the local Adventist church. While she was spending time in Bible classes, I was spending time in the neighborhood bar.

At this point in my life, I was nowhere. I was just existing and trying to find my way. Life was rough after my father left my family when I was seven months old. I called it quits in ninth grade when I was 18 years old, after failing four grades. I became associated with Canada's largest motorcycle gang. I was mainlining and had been doing drugs from the age of 16 to about 19, in addition to drinking heavily. I left the town where I had being living for the past year because a pimp who wanted my girlfriend had threatened my life.

When I arrived in Paris, Ontario I checked in with my brother. He said I could stay at the Christian drop-in center. By this time, I had given up the drugs.

When we met, Kathy and I were both dating other people. However, whenever we saw each other we talked for long periods of time. She felt badly for me and my situation; however, she could not relate at all since we were raised differently. Over time though, we became very good friends.

As time went on, Kathy invited me to go to an Adventist church at a college 100 miles away with her and two of her friends for a special event for young adults. I had arrived home drunk at 3:00 a.m. that same morning before she called to invite me. Having grown up attending church infrequently, I never thought much about religion but I was willing to go since I enjoyed Kathy's company. I dressed in my leather-fringed jacket, purple jeans, yellow shirt and dark gray shades. I didn't even pay attention to the rest of the male congregation, who were all dressed in suits, nor to the minister who delivered a sermon that day on how to dress for church. Kathy did and worried that I would feel uncomfortable but I didn't. After that introduction, I started attending services at the local church and then began to go regularly.

One day during a basketball game, and the excitement of our team making a key basket, I grabbed each of Kathy's pigtails and stared into her eyes. It was surreal, like only the two of us were there. There was some feeling that came between us. She knew it also even though she was unsure what to do with it and if she even wanted it.

My impression of Kathy was that she seemed so full of hope and life was fun for her. She had so much of what I wanted. She was so different from previous girlfriends of mine.

By this point, we had each broken off with our respective partners. On Valentine's Day of that first year, I bought her a cup and saucer made of china. The high quality of china reminded me of Kathy. We kissed that night and after that we started dating.

There were some challenges along the way. For one, Kathy was uncomfortable with our age difference and obsessed about dating me. There appeared to be so many differences, yet she enjoyed my company. She loved the fact that I was a free spirit, opinionated and street-wise.

Eventually Kathy's parents came to visit her in Canada. They knew about me through Kathy's letters and wanted to meet me. Kathy's father liked me, which definitely helped matters. I liked her father so much so that when her parents left, Kathy turned to be comforted by me and was shocked that I was crying. I told her if this is what having a father is like, than I really missed out on a lot.

We continued to date, were engaged at Christmas in England and married the following summer.

Jeanne and Pat

as told by Pat.
Married in 1976 in Stamford, Connecticut.
She was 24; he was 27.

The Hawaiian Vacation

A major corporation located in Stamford, CT arranged a vacation trip. The trip was to Hawaii and many employees were going. My cousin and I arranged to go with a friend who was an employee. Jeanne was going with a friend of hers. Neither Jeanne nor I had been to Hawaii before so we were both excited about the trip.

There were about 60 women and 20 men going for a week to Hawaii. I loved the odds! I headed for the beach once we landed, as did many groups of people. I noticed Jeanne taking off her shorts to sunbathe and was attracted to her shapely figure. Later in the day, everyone started taking part in the activities—dancing, a Don Ho show, etc. On the second day at the beach, I sat with a group of people, which included Jeanne. However, I noticed another guy, who was a fireman, was hitting on her.

The vacation group then traveled to another island and I lost my luggage. I received money to buy new clothes from the airlines and now found the courage to ask Jeanne out. While on the date, Jeanne ordered shrimp and had a bad reaction. Her lips swelled up so bad that they were up to her nose! She asked to be taken back to the hotel. I saw her in the morning and I felt relieved that she looked much better than the previous evening. I asked her out again and she said yes. Later in the day, me being me, I cancelled the date as I received an offer that I felt I could not refuse from another woman. I made an excuse to Jeanne as to why I could not keep the date.

Afterwards I felt so bad about canceling the date but, fortunately, Jeanne reacted relatively well. Friends of hers told her that they thought I really liked her and now she was more interested. The next day we were boarding the plane to return home and the fireman asked Jeanne to sit beside him. I noticed that she looked at him funny and I suggested to her that she sit next to me instead. We talked during the whole flight and ended up holding hands. I told her that I would call her after the trip and, although I waited two weeks to do so, I did call. Jeanne being so understanding, it came as no surprise that she accepted my request to date. We dated for 13 months before marrying.

Riva and Moshe

as told by Moshe.
Married in 1986 in Istanbul, Turkey.
She was 21; he was 22. They divorced in 2005.

In Love Forever

The year was 1979. It was a great summer day when I saw Riva for the first time. She was visiting Prince Island, in Marmara Sea off the shores of Istanbul, Turkey where my family and I spent our summer months. She was like no other 15-year-old girl I had met. She seemed quiet, reserved, simple but also very beautiful. I don't think we exchanged more than a "Hello!"

Fall and the school year came upon us rather quickly, and I was now back in Istanbul. At the time my best friend Miko, who happened to be a schoolmate of Riva's, was telling me how much he enjoyed going to a Jewish Youth Club in our neighborhood. A religious exclusive club seemed a bit separating and one-dimensional to me. I finally decided to give it a try.

I was clearly mistaken. The club, named Yildirim (Thunder), was actually cozy, hip and a safe environment. There were games and sports, day trips and picnics, and dance groups.

It was on the dance floor at the Club where I noticed Riva once again. The reserved, shy beauty, seemed very comfortable among her friends, and lost in the lyrics of the great songs of our time.

Besides the party time, she also was a lead dancer in the Senior Israeli Folklore Group. The dancers often taught the rest of us different dance techniques, by forming mini groups. I made sure I was always in her group to have an opportunity to talk to her and to have physical contact. As I was befriending her, I quickly realized that I was falling in love for the first time in my life.

During the following months we saw more of each other. One day I officially asked her out and after 24 long, torturous hours she delivered her answer, "Yes, but I am scared. I am scared, because you are a womanizer." I was 16 years old at the time.

After five months of beautiful puppy love, Riva was told that her family, like many others, was immigrating to the U.S. in hopes of avoiding the unstable political climate in Istanbul.

We managed to maintain our dating status close to a year and a half by writing letters every day. I lived for every one of them. The following year and a half, the letters became less frequent as we decided to go on with our lives, since our reuniting looked pretty much out of the question.

Yet, on a spring day in 1982 one of those precious envelopes came announcing that she would be coming for a month's visit in the summer to stay with her friend on Prince Island and wanted very much to see me.

The day came and her friend and I picked her up at the airport and went straight to the island. After we spent that beautiful month together we knew we had to somehow be together, forever.

After much planning and strategizing, I came to the U.S. to be with her and we ultimately were engaged on New Years Eve of 1983. We told our parents that we would finish our studies and graduate from college prior to our wedding. Those three years in Santa Barbara were as good as it gets.

The wedding happened in Istanbul with all the pomp and circumstance fitting a "Dynasty era" bash. She was the most beautiful, and happy bride that I had ever seen.

My princess and I remained married for the next 17 years. We worked, we failed, we succeeded, we played, we traveled, we moved nine times to four towns in two states, and had also the most incredible gifts that a couple can have—a daughter and a son.

However in that time, I was battling with a dark secret of my own that I was unable to share with my wife and the rest of the world. I was a gay man slowly coming to terms with his own sexuality. I came out as a gay man and we are now divorced.

Being full and true feels amazing, and in all the turmoil, I had the ultimate love, support and selfless giving of Riva once again. She is my muse and I want to be a better person because of her. We feel strongly that we will remain in each other's lives forever. We now love each other in different ways.

Aisha and John

as told by John.
Married in 2002 in Little Rock, Arkansas.
She was 24; he was 30.

Influential Woman

I was visiting a friend at his house. Aisha drove up and came in to the house. She was my friend's roommate, not his girlfriend. When I saw her I thought to myself, "I got to have that!" I wanted to talk with her but she was leaving just as soon as she arrived. I ran after her and asked if I could call her. She was reluctant. She asked, "Why would I give you my number?" and "Who are you?" I persisted and, finally, she gave me her number.

The next day I called her and arranged to meet her at her house. I went and waited with my friend who was her roommate for three hours. The next night I waited again for about two hours. The next night I waited again. She didn't show. I told myself that was it.

The next day she called me and I asked her what she wanted. She asked me where I felt like going to be with her and I said nothing was open that interested me. She asked if I wanted to go to a room. I agreed. So we met at a hotel room and we talked for a long time, among other things. She asked me to call her and I promised I would and I did.

We started seeing each other often. I was dating a number

of other women, too. Aisha was separated at the time from her husband. I knew that there were other guys she was seeing. After a month though I knew I really was crazy about her. I was getting jealous. She had a great personality and I knew she was good for me.

We decided to discuss all that was happening. I cooked a special meal for her. We talked about our feelings for each other and agreed to be honest with each other. This made us closer.

Unfortunately, due to other circumstances, I ended up in prison at this time. I didn't expect her to wait for me. Most relationships deteriorate with one person waiting for another to be released. Aisha was young and yet she continued to write to me often even though I told her to lead her own life. She even visited with me a few times. She was divorced now.

After I was released, I found out she had lied to me about her seeing other men. I was very upset and disappointed and told her I didn't want to see her again. We argued a lot and talked a lot and argued a lot. This continued until somehow we were able to talk civilly to each other. I realized how much I cared about her. Next, we moved in together. Her mother gave me a very hard time. It was difficult to get a job after being in prison, too. It was a terrible time.

There were a lot of ups and downs due to outside interference in our relationship. My motivation was Aisha. She told me that I had to straighten out my life. She told me to get a job and gave me an ultimatum. I knew how serious she was. I knew that I loved her so much and didn't want to lose her. She was the reason and impetus for me to change. She was pressuring me to marry her and had a bee in her bonnet about it. I confided in my friends who told me that they had lost women by not marrying them. I didn't want to lose her. Our marriage took place about one and a half years after we moved in together.

Rosalyn and Tim

as told by Rosalyn.
Married in 1989 in LaQuinta, California.
She was 30; he was 32. They divorced in 1994.

Long Distance Dating

It was June of 1982. I had just graduated from Law School from the University of Alberta in Canada, and came down to Santa Monica, CA for two weeks to visit my aunt and uncle for a little "R & R" before embarking on my legal career. My uncle is an architect, and he had a young architect moonlighting for him in the evenings named Tim. They thought it would be nice if he might take their young niece out to a movie or dinner while I was visiting. So they invited him out for pizza with us, so that we could meet. After dinner, we came back to their place, and visited and then went into the Jacuzzi and had a drink of Bailey's on the rocks. I was a shy, thin young woman, and had made sure that I was in the Jacuzzi before Tim came in. But once in, I would not leave, as I was too shy to show my bathing suit-clad body. So we stayed in the Jacuzzi for a couple of hours. I was boiling from the heat, and kept hoping that he would get out and leave.

Years later, after we were married, (probably about the time leading up to our divorce), he told me he thought that I was totally smitten with him and just couldn't leave him and, therefore, stayed in the Jacuzzi not wanting him to leave.

Tim was very anxious to ask me out. I wasn't so interested in him. But when he asked me out I thought it would be cool to have a date in California, which I hadn't expected. He wanted to see me every night after that, and it was only about 3-4 days into a two-week vacation. We went out numerous times while I was in California, and we did fun things, including a hike up to the "Hollywood" sign followed by a picnic underneath.

I liked having his attention, but I was actually a little relieved to be getting back to Canada. He was a bit too much to take all at once, and I was just starting my career and was feeling a bit overwhelmed. Well, low and behold, he shows up one week later at the Edmonton International Airport, in July with his long johns on since someone told him it snows all year round in Canada. I couldn't help but admire his persistence. Eventually it tore at my heartstrings and I fell in love.

We had a wonderful long distance romance, meeting in the mountains, San Francisco, Las Vegas, Vancouver, Los Angeles and San Diego. We became engaged to be married one year after we met. Then he got cold feet, even though I had given notice at my job and agreed to move to California. That angered me greatly and I decided to shut him out completely.

I started dating a hockey player whose team participated in the Stanley Cup Finals that year. After Tim recovered from the cold feet thing, he began calling and persisted for over a year. He finally came up to Canada unannounced and was heartbroken since I chose to go to the Stanley Cup Finals rather than see him.

Two years later I moved to Vancouver, and for some reason decided to write Tim a letter. I had recently had a dream about him and wanted to show him that I wasn't such a bad person, and I hoped he was doing well. He took my letter as an open door to start things up, and within a couple of months, he was up in Vancouver to visit me. I believe he wanted to check to see if I hadn't become fat or ugly, after all, this was the first time I had initiated anything. Again, I fell for his persistence, and agreed to move to California six months later. We rekindled whatever feelings there were and started dating again and married soon after.

Cindy and Allen

as told by Cindy.
Married in 2002 in South Lake Tahoe, Nevada.
She was 46; he was 61.

Some People Stay Forever In Our Hearts

When I was a student in high school, there was a teacher named Allen who taught shop. He and his wife taught in the same school, and I was a teacher's aide for his wife. I became friendly with the family and I babysat for their children while he and his wife attended college classes at night.

After graduation from high school, I attended college. Allen contacted me there by letter, asking how my courses were going and how I was getting along in general. We continued to communicate occasionally, through letters and seasonal greeting cards.

After my graduation from college, I moved to a different city, married, and had two children. My family and I moved several times to various locations in Wyoming, and Allen and I continued to write newsy letters of friendship and general interest to each other. He knew of my passion for reading and would also send me books for my birthday and for Christmas.

Eventually, my marriage began deteriorating. My husband and I were finding it more and more difficult to discuss problems and concerns about raising our teenage sons, and I was feeling frustrated about our failure to work together at resolution of family issues.

I continued my communication and friendship with Allen throughout the unhappy years of my marriage. He was very supportive of me through all that I was going through, and became my confidant. He would lift my spirits with his letters of support and encouragement.

Allen's own marriage had been deteriorating, and ended in divorce, after which he moved to the East Coast to complete graduate school.

As I became unhappier in my marriage, and as my children grew older and graduated from high school, I decided to divorce my husband, and begin a new life for myself. I wrote to Allen, and then called him to let him know of my decision. Coincidentally, when I called him, I found out that he had recently broken off his relationship with a girlfriend. He sounded pleasantly surprised that I had finally decided to end my unhappy marriage.

A few weeks later, Allen called to let me know that he was going to be traveling to Wyoming and neighboring states to visit with some family, and asked if he could visit with me. I agreed, and we met for dinner. I had always thought of our relationship as teacher-student, but now felt that he was thinking of me as more than a friend. He then told me that he had loved me for a very long time, but had thought that I would never leave my husband. When he found out that I did, he felt that a dream had come true for him.

After our dinner, Allen traveled on and called me every day. He usually sends postcards to friends when he travels, and, unbeknownst to me, had sent a postcard to friends of his in the Northeast and wrote, "This is the one!"

In February 2002, Allen moved back to Casper, Wyoming, and we married nine months later. We have both been extremely happy with our lives together ever since!

Denise and Ralph

as told by Ralph.
Married in 1982 in Norwalk, Connecticut.
They were both 30.

Oh, How About You and Me?

I met my wife many years ago when we were teenagers. I met her through a former girlfriend of mine when we were riding the city bus in New York. I don't think either one of us knew how many times we would introduce each other to others before we knew we were meant to be.

After we met through my girlfriend, Denise and I dated on and off over the years. Denise had asked me to marry her when we were 18 or 19, but I felt I was not ready so I refused. Despite breakups, we always stayed in touch by continuing to introduce one another several times to others to meet and date.

At one point, I introduced her to a friend of mine and they ended up marrying! The marriage was short-lived and we found ourselves talking again one day at a Mexican restaurant after Denise's divorce to catch up on each other's lives. We had a great time and knew that we wanted to see each other again but, due to our history, we worried it would not last. I even gave Denise her birthday gift a month early since I was afraid our relationship would be over by then. To complicate matters, Denise was working in New York and I was in Connecticut. We therefore decided to do what any couple would do and move in together in Connecticut. We talked of marriage. It was my turn to propose and I did on three different occasions. One occasion was on the Staten Island Ferry and she refused. The next refusal came when I proposed in a doorway in a Greenwich Village shop. I was convinced she wanted me to sweat due to refusing her proposal many years before. Finally she accepted on Christmas Eve when I proposed in our Connecticut apartment.

Once Denise accepted my proposal we invited both sets of parents to our apartment to tell them the good news. They had never met even though they lived five blocks apart in New York for many years. They all arrived at the same time to our apartment and would later become friends.

We planned our wedding with much excitement and anticipation and our friends helped. We had a justice of the peace preside due to our mixed religions. Denise made it special by having both of her parents give her away at the marriage ceremony.

Carmen and Michael

as told by Carmen.
Married in 1991 in Shreveport, Louisiana.
She was 25; he was 29.

Getting It Together

Michael and I met in August 1989, when I visited my cousin at her home in Lynwood, CA. I was five days into my visit when I met Michael at a party hosted by another cousin of mine. My cousin was not very happy with Michael because he had recently broken up abruptly with one of her friends and was now seeing someone else.

Michael and I didn't really hit it off right away, but after a few dances on the dance floor, we sensed some chemistry between us. I thought he was a good-looking guy who was reserved yet fun and shared some of my father's characteristics, which I liked. The following night, we went out to a comedy club in Los Angeles with my cousins and some friends. I had invited an old boyfriend from college who was now living in L.A. to join us, although I was no longer interested in him romantically. I think Michael may have been jealous and this piqued my curiosity in him even more. However, that night at the comedy club, Michael was not the best date and was not very responsive to me. We were both playing hard to get, which we later learned was somewhat attractive to each of us.

The next day, he tried to redeem himself and took me to dinner. During dinner, I agreed to extend my visit for a couple of days so that we could get to know each other a little better. We saw each other every day until I left. He did tell me that I was the most interesting woman he had ever met. I felt that since I was not falling all over him like the rest of the women, he seemed more interested in me. I was interested in him but still had reservations due to what my cousin had told me about his history with women. I expressed my reservations by telling Michael the night before I left to go home, "When you get your shit together, call me." It took only one week for him to get it together. He called me and I was very excited to hear from him. After that, we talked with each other every day and Michael traveled to visit with me over a long weekend in September. I moved to California in November 1989 to be with him, despite my father's reluctance to see me move, and the two of us moved to Atlanta in September 1990 before getting married the following spring.

Julie and John

as told by Julie.
Married in 1990 in Taipei, Taiwan.
She was 33; he was 40.

Getting To Know You

We met due to unforeseen circumstances. John's wife had recently died in a car accident in the U.S. and John was left with a two-year-old to care for. He decided to return to Taiwan with his daughter to find a wife. It was highly desirable for a woman to meet a Taiwanese man living in the U.S. who was educated and had a good job. Therefore, John let some relatives and friends know the reason for his traveling to Taiwan and, since matchmaking is popular with people in Taiwan, the word spread. A number of women communicated their interest in meeting him. I found out through my sister since she had known John's wife.

I was a divorced woman with an eight-year-old daughter. Life in Taiwan for a divorced woman is very limiting as the woman is treated as someone to be avoided. I felt that meeting John might allow my daughter and me an opportunity to get out from under this cloud and provide us a better environment and future.

John arranged to interview quite a few women. John contacted each woman and set up a day and time for each of them to meet him. I was scheduled to be the after-dinner drink on that first day of interviewing. Once he met me he knew this was what he wanted as I was more mature and an experienced, caring mother. John cancelled the rest of the interviews. He wanted to spend more time with me while he was in Taiwan and waited for me to come home from work to visit with me. I made dinner for all of us every day, which he enjoyed. This went on for three weeks.

At this same time I was seeing another man. However, his mother would never allow her son to marry me due to my being divorced and a mother. I had to tell my boyfriend that I was meeting this man. By this point John expressed his interest in marrying me before he returned to the U.S. since he knew intuitively when he met me that I was the one for him.

Two months later John returned from the U.S. to Taiwan to propose to me. I had to tell my boyfriend that I was going to marry John. One month later we married in the city hall and had a big dinner in a fancy restaurant with family and friends.

I wanted to make a happy family for us; however, it was very difficult at first. John and I barely knew each other. He was still in mourning for his first wife. Now that we were living in the U.S., my daughter was having a hard time adjusting to sharing me with others and living in a different country with no extended family support. I cried often. A former Taiwan professor of mine communicated with me regularly and counseled me through this time of adjustment. With family and church support, we are now a happy family.

Don, Nicole, Scott, and Cathy

Nicole and Scott

as told by Nicole.
Married in 1991 in Albuquerque, New Mexico.
She was 22; he was 23.

The Miracle

I met Scott when I enrolled in a computer class. I was sitting in the back and saw Scott walk in. I had noticed him before even though there were 25,000 students on the University of New Mexico (UNM) campus. He was wearing a baseball cap and sat next to me. I pretended that I didn't see him. I started getting confused with a lesson on how to use the computer. Scott leaned over to help me. He had already taken the class before and dropped it, so now he could act like he knew what he was doing. We chatted briefly and flirted with each other. He told me at the end of the class that he was going to be away the next week in Hawaii for a golf tournament. He was on the college team. He also told me that he would bring me something back from his trip.

A few days later on the news, I heard, "Local golfer breaks neck in Hawaii." It was Scott! The news was in the papers and even spread as far as Central America. Scott had just arrived in Hawaii and was running across the beach. He raced into the water to body surf, went head first into the water and went straight down to the bottom of the ocean, hitting his head. He had a compression break. A woman on the beach noticed that he seemed to land in a wrong way. Unbelievably, she was specially trained in spinal injuries and was a lifeguard from Canada on vacation with her husband, Don. Her name was Cathy and this was her last day in Hawaii before returning home. She went straight to Scott and held him up. Cathy had saved him from sustaining permanent injury. She had a team of people form a ring around him to protect him from the waves until an on-duty lifeguard came and then an ambulance arrived. Shortly after, Scott had surgery and was hospitalized in Hawaii for two weeks and then returned home to New Mexico to recuperate. He lived three hours north of Albuquerque and a distance from where I lived and went to school.

I knew he was alive and would be okay but had no way to get hold of him. I went on about my life. I had been feeling lonely and went to church and prayed to God for me to meet someone.

After church, I headed to the library to study. A year after I last saw Scott, we ran into each other at the library. I saw him walk through the library and then he sat right across from me. I was unaware that Scott had enrolled for the fall semester. I was doing research for my course and didn't say anything to Scott but left the table to exchange a book. When I returned to my seat, I found he had left me a note that said how he remembered me from computer class. I looked at him and told him that I remembered him, too. We talked and he said that we should go out sometime. I grabbed his notebook and wrote my phone number on it for him immediately. He called me a few days later and we had our first date. We were engaged ten months later on my birthday and married the next September.

Scott's family always remained in contact with Cathy, the lifeguard. Cathy and her husband have a son named Scott and their son was born on the same day as Scott. We invited Cathy and her husband to our wedding. Our wedding was the first time that Scott and Cathy had seen each other after the accident. At our wedding she read a scripture passage I chose for her. The passage was the same as Cathy had read at her wedding! There have been several more "coincidences" between the two of them since their fateful Hawaiian meeting in 1989. Scott now works as a golf pro at a country club, which is where we had our wedding reception.

chapter four

Childhood Romances

Martha and Carl

as told by Martha.
Married in 1965 in Kanab, Utah.
She was 15; he was 18.

The Grand Adventure of a Lifetime

Carl and I met in high school through my older sister Lydia and her boyfriend Kip. One day Lydia came home from school and asked me if I wanted to go on a blind date with her boyfriend's best friend, Carl. They were going to Carl and Kip's high school baseball game, which sounded interesting. When the boys came to pick us up Carl was driving his brand new Corvair he'd just bought. On the way to the game, Kip and Lydia did all the talking which was fine with me as I was a little shy.

About half way through the game, I was feeling a lot of tension. Carl was very shy and hadn't spoken one word to me yet. Finally out of desperation I asked him the name of the high school they were playing against. He spoke the only words I was to hear from him all night, which were, "I don't know." I wasn't very anxious to go out with him again.

A few weeks later Kip and Carl wanted to take us to our Sunday meetings. I agreed to go out with Carl again in the hope that things would go a little better. Carl drove again and after church the boys wanted to know if we wanted to get a hamburger at Bob's Big Boy, and we did.

After our lunch we went to the car and I noticed Kip getting into the driver's seat and Carl was opening the back door for me. I was feeling a little uneasy as Carl sat next to me. As we were riding I noticed out of the corner of my eye that Carl was staring at me. I turned to look at him and he kissed me. It scared me to death. When Lydia and I arrived home that night, I told her to tell Kip that I didn't want to go out with Carl again.

When Kip told Carl it about broke his heart but I didn't care. One evening my mom was going over to visit my grandmother and I was going with her. Kip was at the house visiting, but I didn't know that Carl had driven him and was sitting out in his car. I walked out to our car, with my mom following. When I saw Carl, my heart sank and not knowing what else to do I stuck my nose up in the air and walked right past him without saying a word! My mother passed him, too. When we were both in our car she said, "Why Martha, you are mean, that boy had tears running down his cheeks!" Hearing her words, I could feel something melt inside of me and I felt really bad.

A few weeks passed and I kind of wanted to make things right between Carl and me. His high school graduation was coming up so I bought him a graduation card and signed it, "Sincerely, Martha." That gave him the courage to ask me out again. Carl and I started dating on a regular basis in May of my freshman year.

I always hated school since I wasn't good at it and would pretend I was sick to get out of going. So I quit school in my sophomore year.

We dated for a year and in that time we learned to love each other as much as kids our age knew how. At 18 and 15 we decided that we were old enough to get married but our parents wouldn't have any part of it. We tried to run away but Carl's mom was watchful and suspected that Carl was up to something.

We wouldn't give up and finally our parents gave their consent.

In the State of Arizona, where we lived, the law said you had to be 16 or pregnant to legally get married so that state was out! Both sets of parents and Carl and I drove to Las Vegas but 16 was the age requirement there also.

My mom did some checking and found that in the State of Utah the legal age was 15. Both sets of parents went before a notary public and they gave their consent for us to go to Utah and get married. Years later I sat talking with my mother and I asked her what ever possessed her to allow me at 15 years old to get married. My mom is a woman of great faith. She said she prayed and asked the Lord if it was right to allow her little girl to get married. His answer to her was a quiet assurance that everything would turn out fine.

At six in the morning on May 25th Carl picked me up at my parent's home. As I gave my mother a hug good-bye I remember thinking to myself, "today I'm going on a grand adventure." Forty years later it hasn't changed. Carl and I are the best of friends besides being sweethearts. We have 10 children of our own and have adopted eight international children with four more on the way!

Unforgettable: Vignettes of Love

Fannie and George

as told by their youngest daughter, Selina.
Married in 1902 in Angoon, Alaska.
She was 16; he was 18. Fannie and George are both deceased.

Keeping Tradition Alive

There was a time when Alaska was a Territory of the United States and records of births and marriages were not recorded with the U.S. Bureau of Vital Statistics, but promises made between two families were kept. Fannie was 13 years old when her family betrothed her hand in marriage to a young man of 15 years named George. At that early age, he already was an accomplished fisherman, hunter, and upstanding Tlingit warrior who was of eligible status to marry the daughter of a Clan Leader (chief) of the Teikweidí (Bear Clan) and sister to a great Clan Leader for the Deisheetaan (Beaver

92

Childhood Romances

Clan). The groom-to-be was of the Eagle moiety or clan and his bride-to-be was from the Raven moiety and according to thousands of years of Tlingit custom and tradition, only the two different moieties could marry. To marry someone from your own moiety was akin to incest and frowned upon by the matrilineal Tlingit of Alaska.

During their betrothal period, their families prepared the young couple for marriage by increasing Fannie's own household items (dowry) while George continued to hone his hunting and fishing skills in order to successfully raise a family in the wilds of Alaska. The two knew each other as they grew up and moved between the fishing villages of Alaska. Their families would come together at fishing and hunting times. They would steal glances at each other when the different villages hosted a ḵoo.éex' (potlatch) or other gatherings.

According to Tlingit custom and tradition, a Tlingit girl was eligible for marriage once she became a woman (menstrual age). So at the young age of 16, Fannie married 18-year-old George in a traditional Tlingit style marriage. His family roots were from Sitka, Alaska a larger village and her roots were in Angoon and when the two finally married in 1902, they made their home in her village of Angoon. Throughout their marriage they had 13 children of which seven reached adulthood amidst the hardships and ravishes of raising children in remote Alaska.

They respected each other and shared similar high morals and values. Each admired the other for their skills to provide for their family, be it hunting or making moccasins. George and Fannie remained married for 62 years. He died six years after Fannie but their youngest daughter, who is now 77 lives to tell their story, along with George and Fannie's 45-plus direct descendants who are thriving in the 49th State of Alaska to this day, where Tlingit customs and traditions are resurging but betrothed marriages remain a thing of the past.

Winnie and Winston

as told by Winnie.
Married in 1946 in Keene, New Hampshire.
She was 22; he was 30. Winston died in 2003.

The Most Beautiful Girl

We both grew up in Chesterfield, New Hampshire. There was a combination grocery store/Post Office where Winston worked. I was only twelve years old and remember my family ordering groceries from the store. Winston would always have our order ready when I would come to pick it up. We would never talk.

As I became older I became known as "the most beautiful girl in Chesterfield." Every week I would go to Brattleboro with my brother to go dancing. Winston would go also with his friends, but he didn't dance. One night he told my brother to ask me if I wanted to go out with him. My brother told him to ask me himself. He asked me out but I refused him twice. Everyone liked him and I thought he was nice-looking but I was unsure of dating him. He told himself that he would ask me out only one more time. Then he would look elsewhere. This time I accepted and we went to a movie. We started dating.

After we dated over two years, Winston took me to Brattleboro for one of our regular trips. He told me to go to the jewelry store and I said, "Why?"

He said, "You are going to marry me, aren't you?"

I said, "Yeah, I guess," and he bought me an engagement ring. We married two months later. Winston always said that he knew we would marry.

Edith and Sid

as told by Sid.
Married in 1999 in Beckley, West Virginia.
She was 69; he was 72.

Never Too Late

I met Edith when a mutual friend of ours took me to Edith's locker in high school to introduce me. We immediately liked each other and dated for about two years. We thought we would marry but it didn't happen since I went off to college in another state and we drifted apart. I would come home on the weekends and drive by her house occasionally but we lived different lives. Edith met someone and married when she was 19 years old. I met someone and married in my junior year of college. My wife and I had three children, as did Edith and her husband. In 1997 my wife became ill and passed away. I have never been the type of guy to be single and wished to meet someone.

I thought of Edith from time to time and wondered what it would have been like if we had married. I decided to see if I could find Edith.

I was still living in another state but on one of my trips home, I went to the county courthouse and found her married name and address. I thought I would give her a call and, if she were still married, I would invite her and her husband to dinner.

I called Edith on three different occasions before someone finally answered. We talked for a while and then I told her I would be visiting in a few weeks and asked if she and her husband would go to dinner with me. She told me her husband had passed away (the year before my wife had.) Once I knew that she was willing to see me, I called her back in a few days and told her that I would be down to visit that weekend. When I arrived at her house and approached her door, she stuck out her hand to greet me. After 50 years, I said I wanted a hug!

We went to a Chinese restaurant for dinner and both became ill from the food. We took turns using the bathroom while we were in the restaurant but wanted to continue our conversation.

I visited Edith the next day at her house. Her daughter was there and eyed me with suspicion. She asked me what my intentions were for her mother. Edith and I knew that we wanted to be with each other and didn't have to recreate our feelings for each other. They were always there.

I was involved in volunteer activities and worked part-time where I was living. Once I settled my business and personal matters, I moved back to Beckley and Edith and I married three months later.

After three years of marriage, Edith fell ill with cancer. I nursed her back to health. We now travel and enjoy our time together.

Tricia and Mike

as told by Mike.
Married in 1992 in Omaha, Nebraska.
She was 24; he was 23.

I Only Have Eyes For You

Tricia and I met when we were very young — she was 14 and I was 12. It was 1982. Our parents both owned sailboats on a lake in South Dakota. She was from Iowa and I was from Nebraska and every summer we would see each other at the lake. We became friends over the years and eventually our friendship grew stronger. When I was about 15, I realized that Tricia was not only my best friend but also someone I was interested in romantically. She was beginning to develop feelings for me, too. In the beginning, it was a trying time for us since our two-year age difference and the long distance between our homes held us back from seeing each other as often as we wished. She was in high school doing high school things like being a cheerleader, going to proms and homecomings. I was in junior high wondering what I was missing. However, we always made an effort to maintain the relationship.

A couple years passed and it was time for Tricia to start thinking about what college to attend. It was then that I felt like I had to step it up a notch and help her with some suggestions. I feared nothing more than for her to go to college in some state far away. This would have made things even harder for us to see each other. I thanked my lucky stars that she decided upon a college in Omaha, Nebraska, with a little help from me, perhaps. Now, for the first time, we were in the same city and not seeing each other just on the weekends or during the summers.

She was a college freshman and I was a junior in high school. All my friends had heard about this "mystery girl" for the past five years. It certainly didn't hurt my popularity telling my friends that Tricia was a college girl and the head of the Pom Squad. Some, more than likely, thought that I was making up some dream girl. I was finally able to ask her to my high school proms and of course she said yes. Now everyone could meet her.

When I graduated from high school I chose the college that Tricia was attending, much to my parents' dismay since it was a very expensive school. I will always be grateful to my parents for letting me attend, although I am sure they knew that I chose the school due to Tricia's being there. Once Tricia graduated, I switched to a more affordable school for my last two years of college.

We married in 1992. It is hard to believe that I have had only one love all this time. It's even harder to believe I met my wife when I was 12. Don't let anyone say you can't marry your first love. You can and I did.

Mena and Ted

as told by Mena.
Married in 1999 in Thomaston, Connecticut.
She was 61; he was 60.

The Wish of Two Mothers

I remember Ted was a new eighth-grade student. I was smitten at first sight. The one memory that has lasted through the years was our being squished in the backseat of Ted's best friend's aqua-green convertible while our friend drove a number of classmates home from school. Ted tried to ask me out several times but we were both too shy to communicate.

We graduated from high school and proceeded to lead different lives. I married very young, had five children, became a nurse and divorced after 10 years of marriage. Ted went on to become a fighter pilot and then a commercial airline pilot.

The only time I saw Ted after high school was when I was with my children and a girlfriend at Nystroms Pond when we were 19. He walked by but didn't stop since he felt it was improper for a single man to approach married women.

In later years, I moved back with my mother and cared for her until she died. It was a rough time accepting her death and I had a difficult time adjusting. Nothing seemed to help except the long walks I took every day after work. One day while walking, I suddenly entered our local church even though I had not been to church for 30 years. Alone in the dim light, I knelt and cried. During this time, I told God I was so unhappy, that I felt so alone and miserable all the time.

I left the church that day, drained and exhausted. Very soon after, things began to happen where each day brought something to give me a bit of sunshine in my heart.

My mother's passing was reported in the local paper. I followed up the report with a letter in the paper praising my parents for my upbringing. Although Ted lived out-of-state, he received the local paper. He noticed my letter and sent me a note to the only address he knew—my mother's house. His note expressed his sorrow and also informed me of his mother's death two weeks before mine.

I decided to write back to Ted. I tore up the first seven or eight letters I wrote, until, at last, with my heart in my throat, I finally sent one.

He answered. I answered, and we began to exchange letters. In one of the letters, Ted sent me a picture of a barn behind his former house. I went to the house to look for the barn. One of my coworkers now lived in the house and had been there for 28 years. I talked about Ted and this unfulfilled love I had for him. My coworker remembered something she had found when she first moved in the house and was gardening in the yard. It was a wedding ring and she gave it to me.

Ted and I were in constant communication and our letters grew warmer and more eagerly anticipated. We were able to know each other as adults. I let Ted know that I had been given something from his old house but that it would be best given to him in person.

We arranged for him to visit Thomaston after his many years away to come see me. I was terrified. Forty years is such a long time to carry a memory. The day arrived and when I opened the door, we looked across 40 years and the time vanished, somehow.

All this time, Ted had lived his life as a confirmed bachelor. The next night as we were sitting together, I gave Ted his mother's platinum wedding ring!

On my birthday, June 1, Ted took me back to Nystroms Pond, the last place where our eyes had met. It was there that he proposed, using his mom's ring for the "engagement" ring. By this time, I had found my mother's engagement ring and continue to wear that, too.

As I waited for my cue to walk down the aisle on our wedding day, I was almost in tears and said to my daughter, I wish my mom and dad could be here now. At that moment a very heavy door on the side of the church near where I was waiting slowly opened and slowly closed. No one visible came in but a light caress of a breeze passed over me. My daughter jumped for the door to see if anyone was out there. No one was. She closed the door, and said to me, with tears in her eyes, "They're here, Mom," and I proceeded tearfully but joyously down the aisle.

We feel that this is the gift of two mothers to their two children so they can get on with enjoying heaven, knowing their children are now safe, loved, and not alone anymore.

chapter five

Parental Involvement

Linda and Michael

as told by Linda.
Married in 1967 in Mt. Isa, Queensland, Australia.
She was 21; he was 23.

Overcoming Distance and Differences

I was just 16 and very shy. It was the first day of my first job in an office of a department store in Ipswich. I was taken around and introduced to all the staff and in the dispatch section was this good looking young man who looked very much like my idol, "Elvis Presley." His name was Michael.

We would cast our eyes in each other's direction whenever we saw each other over the next few months and occasionally stop to chat. Then one day he asked me to go and watch him play football. That was when we began dating regularly.

However, fate stepped in and Michael lost his job through a football injury. His only recourse at the time was to head to Mt. Isa 1,200 miles away where his sister lived to find work. He would live there for 12 years. We communicated by letter for several months then lost touch.

Two years after he first went to Mt. Isa, he was back in Ipswich for holiday. To my disbelief, we bumped into each other crossing the street at the shopping center! We talked for a long time and he asked me out. By the end of his three-month holiday, he had given me a friendship ring thus committing us to each other.

For the next two years our courtship was by letters sent every day and twice yearly visits either by my going to Mt. Isa or Michael's coming to Ipswich. On New Year's Day in 1967 Michael proposed marriage and that is when the problems with our families began.

Our parents objected to our marriage as we came from different religious backgrounds. Neither set of parents would attend a wedding not in the church of their denomination.

After 10 months of heartache trying to sort this out, my stepfather in his wisdom suggested we go off and do our own thing. So I "eloped" to Mt. Isa and a week later Michael and I were married in a church with four people in attendance. I was given away by a workmate of Michael's whom I had only known for one week. His wife was my matron of honor. There were just the four of us at a restaurant for our reception. It was a fantastic wedding and about which we have no regrets. We took our vows with as much commitment to each other as we would have had if the church had been full of family and friends. We are as much in love today as ever.

Ruth and Charles

as told by Ruth.
Married in 1945 in a small Illinois town.
She was 25; he was 27. Charles died in 1959.

Three Times A Charm!

My mother owned a luncheonette in New York City at the time. One of her regular customers was a guy from Illinois named Charles. He taught medical courses at Cornell Medical School in the City. My mother talked about him and how he would eat French crullers all the time just like my stepfather.

One day I waited on him when he came into the luncheonette. I was immediately attracted to him. We talked and he asked me to a movie. Afterwards, he wanted to go for ice cream at Schraft's but I suggested we go elsewhere. I walked with him the long way back to mother's luncheonette. While we were eating ice cream he told me he had to tell me something. I said, "Please don't tell me that you are married." He said he was! I had been dating two different guys right before I met Charles and found out that each of them was married. I was so upset. He explained that his wife walked out on him and that they would be divorcing by the end of the year. Despite my disappointment, I decided to believe him and chance it since he sounded sincere. We kept company and Charles fell hard for me. His marriage ended as he said it would.

My mother ended up not liking him since he didn't try to flatter her as others had. She kept asking me, "Are you still serious about this guy?" I was so annoyed at this question being asked all the time that I said, "There is one thing you must know. I am marrying this guy—get used to it!"

Since this was wartime, Charles was called for his physical. He passed and was selected for the Navy. He went back to Cornell to tell the dean of the medical school where he taught and the dean said he couldn't go to war. At that time, the medical school was training doctors for the war and the instructors were needed. The dean immediately picked up the phone and starting dialing phone numbers with Charles by his side. Within a few minutes, Charles knew that the dean was being transferred to different people. Finally, the dean said, "Franklin, you can't let Charles be in the Navy. You will have to close the school if he is." It was President Franklin Delano Roosevelt and Charles was released from military duty.

We planned on marrying over Labor Day. My mother's sisters were fighting, so in order to avoid any displays at the wedding, my mother asked if we could marry in Charles' hometown in Illinois instead. Charles told his mother and we made arrangements. Then my parents and I flew to Illinois for our wedding. Once married Charles and I lived very happily.

Marilyn and Frank

as told by Marilyn.
Married in the 1980s in Spartanburg, South Carolina.
She was in her 30s; he was in his 40s.

The Boys Next Door

Once I graduated from college I moved to different areas of the Midwest for my career. I was a microbiologist. I met a guy and married but after giving birth to our daughter, I realized that the marriage was not to last. My parents worried about my being a single mother and wanted me to move back to my hometown where they lived. However, I wanted to establish myself and demonstrate that I could take care of my daughter and myself.

My mother really wanted me to move back home and pestered me to call a local contact from a company that my mother thought would hire me. I finally relented, called the company, had an interview scheduled and was offered a position. I had to settle all of my affairs in a two-week time period and move back to South Carolina. I managed to do so even with flying back and forth from Chicago to settle personal and professional matters.

On one of my trips home I had to look for a place to live. When I was with my realtor looking at houses, I noticed a blue house for sale, which had a mailbox with the same last name as mine. I felt it was meant for me to see. With only one day to make a decision before I returned to Chicago, I chose the blue house.

Once I moved in I met two young boys who lived next door, ages eight and 12. They liked visiting my daughter and me and were over all the time. Then all of a sudden they didn't show for a few days. I wondered where they were and when they returned I asked what happened. They said they were ill and I became concerned from their looks that they were not properly cared for. I knew that they lived with their father, Frank, and that he was going through a divorce. I had met him briefly after I moved in.

I invited them all to dinner so they could have a home-cooked meal. The dinner went very well and Frank, for all intents and purposes, never left. After dinner he helped me with a project I had going on in the backyard. In the days following the dinner, we started working on different home projects and enjoyed our time together. We never went on a date as we always had the children with us.

After three years, everyone knew that we enjoyed being with each other and they wanted us to marry. Even my ex-mother-in-law wanted us to marry! I was not so sure. My daughter knew of my reluctance and played off of the fact that Frank was shorter than I by telling me, "Mommy, even short people need love."

One day Frank asked me if I wanted to accompany him on a business trip to Europe. I did. Frank told me that he thought we should be married if we were to go. He sold me on the idea and we set a date to coincide with the upcoming trip. We designed invitations that had the names of our three children on them in place of our parents' names. Once we married my daughter wanted so much to have Frank as her father that she asked her new brothers if it was okay for her to call their father, "Dad." Frank moved ahead and adopted my daughter. She also wanted a sister, which we were able to produce a few years later!

Delanie and Greg

as told by Greg.
Married in 1993 in Sun Valley, Idaho.
She was 37; he was 39.

Standing Out In The Crowd

We met at an Elks Lodge dance in Boise, Idaho on a Sunday night in July 1992. I came with a male friend and Delanie was with her mother who was single. My friend and I had been riding our motorcycles through the Sawtooth Mountains of Idaho all weekend and I was really tired. My friend wanted some social interaction with people other than me, which meant f-e-m-a-l-e. I wanted him to go home and leave me alone. I had a nice life as a single parent of a preteen boy who was visiting his mother for two weeks and wanted some peace and quiet. I had no interest in additional social interactions that day.

When we arrived at the Elks Lodge I realized that we were two of only a few people there under the age of sixty. I saw Delanie with her mother and asked her to dance. I thought she was beautiful! I thought initially that she had smiled at me from across the room, but found out later she was interested in the guy standing behind me next to the wall. We had one dance together and she went and sat down with her mother. The other guy asked her to dance and she spent the rest of the night dancing with him. So I did the next best thing and sat with her mother until I left with my friend. We talked the whole time about Delanie. Once I was leaving I was able to get Delanie's work phone from her mother. I called her the following week and set up a lunch date with her. It went so-so. Next I asked her for an evening date to go dancing and picked her up at her home. I knew that she was dating a number of guys during this time and wondered what number date I was that day.

The evening date went okay. I stepped on her feet several times since I'm not a good dancer, but I didn't revolt her. I asked her for a third date which she agreed to. At his point, I spent most nights and weekends with my son. I felt it was better to build a friendship first with Delanie. She gradually dumped the other guys and told me that she respected my honesty, integrity and generosity. We also knew that we shared the same family values. Delanie and I dated about once a week or so until November. Then things became more serious and we married a year later.

Heeki and Rejun

as told by Heeki.
Married in 2002 in Kitakyushu, Japan.
She was 29; he was 28.

Getting Through Customs

I met Rejun when I was 20 and going to school in California. I had never had a boyfriend, which one of my friends thought was quite rare and decided to do something about it. My friend knew Rejun's cousin, and between the two of them, arranged for us to meet at the car wash the cousin owned.

Rejun had just returned from Japan when we met. He asked me out and we went to a Japanese restaurant since we thought it would be cool to have a sushi date in the U.S. I thought he was very gentle and a nice young man. We started seeing each other in a dating relationship.

Rejun came from a very conservative Korean-Japanese family. He was the first son of four children and he knew that he would have to take over the family business in the future. He had been sent to the U.S. for a better education and to prepare for his role as the heir. Since he was seven years old, his parents had told him he must marry a person whom they would chose. During our years of dating, he was actually forced to meet a number of girls that his parents chose through matchmakers. He rejected all of them.

The trigger for us to marry was when Rejun's father found out I existed. Rejun was in Japan working for his father in the family business, and after I graduated from UCLA I flew to Japan to see him. When his father found out about me he went crazy with anger. Rejun's mother and grandma were our saviors. They wanted me to come to their house to see what I was like. So I went, and we talked for several hours about the circumstances and customs and my Korean background. Finally, Rejun's grandma said, "If you want to marry Rejun, you have to live together with us at our house. That is our family rule because Rejun is the first son. Is that okay?" I said, of course, "No problem."

How could I say "no" in that situation? For all intents and purposes they approved of me and they persuaded Rejun's dad to let us marry. Finally, after we had dated eight years, we married.

Renee and Paul

as told by Renee.
Married in 1946 in Yonkers, New York.
She was 22; he was 26.

Permission Granted

I met my husband Paul through one of my brothers. He and my brother were friends. I was one of eight children and there were always friends of ours coming to our house. One day Paul showed up. I was immediately attracted to him and was very happy that he asked me out. It was traditional in an Italian family for the daughter to ask permission of her father if she was asked out on a date. So I told Paul I would have to ask my father to be able to go. He understood since he was of Italian descent, too. Fortunately my father gave his consent since he had met Paul that same day and liked him. Our first date was to a movie.

World War II broke out a few months later and by that time we were dating on and off. Paul was drafted and went off to war. He was based in Fort Bragg, North Carolina. When he would come home on the weekends, we would go out on dates. We did this for two years and by that time I had met his parents and he was a part of our family, too. On his last visit home before being sent overseas, Paul gave me a diamond as an engagement ring. Once again, I had to tell him that I had to ask my father if I had permission to accept the ring and his marriage proposal. I was so grateful that my father gave his consent.

Paul then went off to Hawaii, then Guam, and the Philippines and on to Okinawa. He was wounded slightly and awarded the Purple Heart. He wrote letters to me and also sent packages. My mother would make raviolis and preserve them and send them to Paul. When the war ended in 1945, Paul stayed in Japan to support a campaign as part of the post-war effort for four to five months. After he returned on December 15, 1945, he looked for employment. We felt it was important for him to be employed before we married but it was difficult to find a job since all the men were returning from the War. We went ahead and married anyway the following May.

Parental Involvement

Nwaka and Emeka

as told by Emeka.
Married in 1999 in Ozitem, Abia, Nigeria and Lagos, Nigeria.
She was 29; he was 30.

Honoring Customs

It was Labor Day weekend 1997 in Washington, D.C. and I had flown in from Atlanta to attend the wedding of a friend to be held the next day. I arrived at a friend's house where a number of other attendees had gathered for the customary co-ed Bachelor's Eve party. Soon after, I volunteered to pick up a friend arriving at the airport. As I was leaving I saw this woman come out from the kitchen. I was taken aback by the way she looked and knew that I had to meet her. I asked some of my friends who she was and they told me her name was Nwaka. Then I went and introduced myself.

She looked perfect. She told me that I was so considerate and sweet to offer to pick up our friend. I told her not to leave because I would be right back.

When I returned to the house we chatted and had a good time. I learned Nwaka was in the U.S. to attend graduate school. Later that evening both of us eyed each other when we were talking with others. The next day at the wedding reception we found ourselves assigned to the same table and sat next to each other. We had attention only for each other that day.

After the wedding, we started dating by talking on the phone for long periods of time and commuting to see each other. In 1998 we began talking seriously about marriage. Nwaka called her mother on New Year's Eve in 1999 to wish her a happy New Year. I had never met her mother but took the phone and told her mother that I was marrying her daughter. Nwaka told me later that she loved that I took such a bold, devilish move and considered me a "keeper." I knew that Nwaka was leaving that month to go to Nigeria and I wanted to make our intent to marry official.

Our discussing marriage meant we had to get our families involved who were both living in Nigeria. I contacted my family to tell them of our wish to marry. Then, I contacted her father to ask his permission. Our coming from the same tribe made things easier since we had the same traditions and understandings.

In Nigerian culture, it is the role of the males in each family to negotiate for the wedding. So the next step was the traditional "knocking at the door," that would take place in Nigeria. This is the introduction where the groom-to-be's family comes to the house of the bride-to-be and says, "The reason that we are here is that our son found something good in this house. Is she available?" The groom-to-be's family also brings a traditional gift with them, such as, a bottle of whiskey.

It is the whole family's decision whether or not the couple can marry. For instance, the male head of the village decides the size of the material dowry, which, in our case, was made up of fabric, food and schnapps. Nwaka's uncles, grandfather and father negotiated the types of animals and other goods that were important to bring to the bride's family. The more serious negotiations lasted from January to March. Overall, about one dozen people were involved.

During this time, Nwaka and I were nervous and worried since nothing is guaranteed until the wedding day. By custom, we should not say anything but we each let our parents know that we *really* wanted the negotiations to go well so we could marry.

I presented Nwaka with an engagement ring when she returned from Nigeria in January. While the negotiations were ongoing in our homeland, we moved ahead with the U.S. plans about who to invite, who would be our attendees, etc.

We first married in a village ceremony, which is the traditional custom. A week later we held our church ceremony. Since we were the first son and daughter in our respective families to marry, we had a huge turnout for our wedding: 2,500 people. It was held at the National Arts Theatre in Lagos so all of our guests could be accommodated in the large ballroom.

After it was all over, we realized we were exhausted from the year's events and decided to cancel our honeymoon to Switzerland. We returned to Atlanta where Nwaka had moved to live with me and start our life together.

Trudy and Trace

as told by Trace.
Married in 1989 in Charlotte, North Carolina.
She was 23; he was 30. They divorced in 2005.

The Runaway Couple

I met Trudy when she was five years old. I played Little League with her brother in Fort Myers, Florida. I remember her throwing spitballs at the back of my head when her brother and I walked to the baseball field.

Years later, after I had been dating a number of women, I declared that I wanted a fresh life and a new woman. I moved into a new apartment complex. Shortly after, a former girlfriend telephoned me and suggested we go to a luau being held at the complex the following weekend. I was reluctant to go but let her know that I was looking for a new woman in my life. When we arrived at the luau, my former girlfriend bet me that I wouldn't dance with anyone. I said, "Point a woman out and I will go and ask her to dance." She pointed out an attractive woman and I went over and asked her to dance. We danced, chatted and started dating. I didn't recognize her at first but realized shortly after meeting her that this was Trudy who I had known since she was a little girl! She was dating someone else at the time, even though she came to the luau with girlfriends.

We continued to date even while Trudy continued to date the other guy. Trudy felt she couldn't tell her boyfriend that she wasn't interested in him anymore, so one day when he came by the house, I did it for her. We then moved in together. After a year we talked about marriage. Her parents wanted a big, grand wedding but we did not. We drove to her parents' vacation home and started our search for a minister to marry us. Everyone that we spoke with told us we shouldn't be eloping and that we should return home and go see a counselor. Finally after five days we found a Baptist minister to marry us, even though he didn't like our idea. We drove back to Florida and announced our marriage to our family, letting them know that we had our honeymoon before our wedding.

Heliz and Renas

as told by Renas.
Married in 1987 in Kurdistan, Iraq.
They were both 19.

Love Thy Neighbor

I lived in the same village as Heliz. It was a small village and we would see each other from time to time. We started talking with each other one day and did so again, infrequently. After I saw Heliz, I went to my father and told him that I wanted to marry her. My father said, "If you like her it was okay. If you don't, don't bother with her." I told my father that I really liked Heliz. My father went to Heliz' house and he told her father that I wanted to marry his daughter. Her father told my father that it was okay even if Heliz didn't love me because we were neighbors so we would marry. However, Heliz's father did ask her how she felt about me. She said she loved me.

Once we knew that we would marry, I spoke to Heliz's father and asked what she needed. I bought her the wedding dress, the ring and a necklace for the wedding as her father expected that I would buy his daughter these things. We had to wait one year though to marry since my father passed away. After the wedding we didn't go on a honeymoon since it is not part of our tradition. We moved in with my mother. We wanted to help my brothers and sisters, financially, due to my father's passing.

Karen and Chris

as told by Karen.
Married in 1996 in Portland, Oregon.
She was 32; he was 33.

Conventional Resistance

My husband and I met in Chicago. I was 23 and a theatre technician/scenic carpenter at the time. I was called to The Goodman Theatre to sub for Chris, one of their grips or spotlight operators. I was to meet him backstage before a performance. When I arrived, someone pointed him out as "The guy in the pony tail over there." His back was to me, and he was tall, lean, and broad-shouldered with strong lean arms, and quite a nice butt, all very appealing to me. I tapped him on the shoulder. He turned and fixed me with incredibly blue eyes. And when he smiled, deep dimples on his cheeks and crinkles about his eyes made me smile, too.

As he trained me over the next few days, I could tell he was interested in me, and I was reluctant to tell him I was dating someone, but I felt it was only fair. So when we were up in the catwalks chatting between spotlight cues, I casually slipped in the phrase "my boyfriend." Out of the corner of my eye, I saw him physically deflate.

A year later, I agreed to be a grip for a season at the Chicago Opera Theatre. When I was setting up the scenery, a tall, skinny guy running around like a madman in charge of electrics caught my attention. Something was excitingly familiar about him. It was Chris.

I was the only girl on the stage crew that season, with the exception of the costumers. Most of the male crew seemed to be mate-less, so I was hit on incessantly by them all—except Chris. He'd casually hang around and play backgammon with me between scenes. It finally dawned on me, as he was master electrician, once the show was up and running, he had no need to be there during performances. He was there because of me and I was currently unattached!

During one performance, I fell down the backstage cement staircase. The production manager gave Chris the company car to take me to the hospital. I was all right, but the doctors ran some tests to make sure, and in the meantime my parents showed up. My father asked who brought me in. I told him it was the guy out in the waiting room and asked him to send Chris in to me. My father went out, came back in, and said, "There's nobody out there but some guy in an army jacket with long hair and an earring."

I said, "That's Chris! Tell him to come in here."

My dad went out, came back in and said, "I told him to go home."

I said, "Dad, go get him and tell him to come in here!" My dad shook his head, went out, told him to go home, and came back in. I was about to have it out with my dad when Chris walked in with a smile on his face that told me he clearly knew what my father was up to, came over to me, asked me how I was, and, much to my parents' chagrin, kissed me and said, "I'll see you tomorrow." I was stunned and impressed he didn't let my father push him around, and stunned and delighted he kissed me, as we hadn't even gone on a date yet!

My dad should have known right then and there, this was the man I was going to marry, if for no other reason because he felt it was the last man on earth I should marry.

We moved in together less than a year after that, and three years later moved to Oregon. We considered ourselves married and felt no need to have to "prove it to the state" or get the state's approval. After eight years together we had our first daughter. (When I told my father he would be a grandfather, he asked, "So are you going to make it legal?" I told him it was legal in Oregon to have a baby.) The only reason we "legally" married was to satisfy Chris's new employer's requirement of a marriage certificate for medical insurance to cover the whole family.

We married on a lovely summer day on the shores of Clear Lake up in Mt. Hood, with just our Oregon friends in attendance. We had separate receptions for friends and family back in the Midwest.

Since our wedding we have had another daughter and our parents have forgiven us our ways because their granddaughters are very cute, very engaging, and love their grandparents very much.

Thelma and Luis

as told by Luis.
Married in 2000 in Long Island, New York.
She was 45; he was 38.

Are You Ready?

Thelma was living in San Salvador, the capital city of El Salvador and was widowed at an early age. She had two children to care for. My mother had known Thelma and had cared for her when Thelma was a little girl. My mother suggested that Thelma have her children live with us so we could care for them while Thelma found work in the big city to support them. Thelma would join us at my mother's house each weekend in our small town.

When I met Thelma I was immediately attracted to her and she to me. We talked with each other a lot and enjoyed each other's company. We never told anyone of our attraction since she was much older than I and she felt that my mother would object. She also felt I should have my own family with someone who had not been married before. After a few years Thelma decided to move to New York. I realized as soon as she left that I missed her very much and wanted to be with her. I called her and she was very happy to hear from me and could not wait for me to get to New York! To our surprise, my mother didn't object but was very happy since she always loved Thelma.

We continued to work to get her children with us and after two years they joined us in New York. When we started living together Thelma would ask me about marriage and I would always say I was not ready. Then her questions stopped. The years went on and I began to realize how uncomfortable I felt when I would have to refer to Thelma as my partner, the person I live with, my girlfriend, etc. and how disrespectful it was to her. Finally I suggested to Thelma that we marry. She was so excited. After 15 years we married with her two children as the witnesses at our wedding!

Mandy and Scott

as told by Scott.
Married in 1997 in Tuscaloosa, Alabama.
She was 21; he was 25.

Father Knows Best

Mandy had started working in the local bakery and deli store. She had just moved from Millport to Tuscaloosa and was in her junior year of high school.

I was having a hard time. A two-year relationship broke up and I was devastated. On top of that, my mother had just had surgery. In order to survive and since my father and I were not the best of cooks, my father would stop at the bakery and deli for food for our meals. While there, he would stop and talk with Mandy. One day he came home and told me that he met a cute girl and suggested that I ask her out. I was a little shy and I didn't want my dad to set me up and I felt I could do it on my own when I was ready. After more prodding from my father though, I relented.

What we didn't know was that my father and the owner of the store were conniving to get us together. They told Mandy that I would be stopping by. Upon seeing her, I thought she was cute right away and probably older than she was. I found out later she was only 17. I said, "Hey, how are you?" I sat down after giving my order and asked her to sit with me. She took a break so she could be with me. We chatted about our lives and I stayed to help her with chores to close the store. I then walked her to her car and asked her out for that Saturday. She said, "You're talking to me?" I said, "No one else is standing here!" Fortunately she thought I was cute and sweet and she accepted. I found out later that three other guys were interested in her but she refused all of them.

I was very nervous going to pick her up since I had to meet her parents. The owner of the store had told me that Mandy's father is tough and carried a gun. I did not know the owner was joking. I knocked on the door and saw her father was sitting in the living room. Luckily her parents were very nice and I didn't see any guns. I was told to have her in by 11:00 p.m. They all laughed when I showed my age by telling them that the parents of the last girl I dated told me to bring her home when I finished with her!

I was excited to have met Mandy and strongly liked her after our date. We had a lot in common and even found out that our grandfathers worked at the same plant and they knew each other. When I was dropping her at home after our date, I wanted to kiss her. I leaned toward her and asked if I could see her ring and then I kissed her! She must have liked it because she asked if I wanted to come by the next day. We dated for the next five years.

During our years of dating, I created a scrapbook of many of our photos from our dates and the different places we visited. The scrapbook was not complete. At the end of the book there was a letter that I had written to Mandy. The letter stated that in order to make our scrapbook complete, she would have to answer a question for me. I gave her a card and inside the card was a question: Mandy, would you marry me? I then looked at her and said the words, to her shock and surprise. She luckily replied yes and we married 2 ½ years later.

Kristina and Joe

as told by Kristina.
Married in 2000 in Chagrin Falls, Ohio.
She was 28; he was 29.

When East Meets West

I was student teaching for a semester at a nearby school close to my home. My boyfriend had given me an engagement ring and I was either too scared or too unsure if he was the right person so I broke up with him. I was feeling really lonely and wanted to meet someone since all my friends were getting married.

I was in my room moping and my mother came in to comfort me. While hugging me and assuring me that I would meet another guy, she said, "I just have a feeling that he is right around the corner."

I was from the East side of town. A friend of mine suggested that we try this bar that I had never been to which was located on the West side of town in Lakewood. While at the bar, a guy named Joe noticed me and sent over a drink. On the way out I went over to thank him. He said he would like to see me again and asked me out to dinner. I accepted even though I wasn't sure I wanted to go. When we met for dinner I was immediately attracted to him. He looked great without the baseball cap he had on when we first met! We dated, fell in love and married. The name of the bar where we met was "Around the Corner Saloon and Café"!

chapter six

Looking for Mr. and Mrs. Right

Barbara and Walt

as told by Barbara.
Married in 1970 in Stamford, Connecticut.
She was 22; he was 24.

The Ouija Board Knows

Walt noticed me at the local bar where everyone hung out at that time, although he never talked to me. He did remember me from high school and decided to call me up for a date. I remembered him as being in the class two years ahead of mine. When I returned home from the date, my mother said that I didn't ask her, "How do you know when you are in love" anymore. All I said was how terrific and grownup he was. She knew he was the one. We were married one year from our first date.

Two years earlier while in my college dorm, I was playing with the Ouija Board and I asked whom I was going to marry. The board said "wu-wu." It repeated "wu-wu" every time I asked the same marriage question. I found out after we dated that Walt's nickname in high school was "Wu-Wu"!!

Irene and Bill

as told by Irene.
Married in 1980 in Carmel, California.
She was 34; he was 40.

The Kiss

My husband and I met when he joined the company I worked for, a real estate investment firm in the San Francisco Bay Area. We were both single at the time, although I was involved with someone I had been dating for several years.

I'll never forget the first time I saw him. I saw one of the partners coming down the stairs in front of our office building, accompanied by a good looking guy. My first thought was that this must be the new guy and he is very cute. He paid no attention to me. His name was Bill.

Over the next two years, I was aware of Bill since he rose up the corporate ladder pretty quickly. That didn't mean that I had a very high opinion of him though, because he was quite a lady's man and seemed to cut a wide swath through many of the single females in the company.

In 1979, the relationship I was involved in ended amicably. About that time, I was getting restless in the job I had been doing for the past eight years and wanted a change, but didn't want to leave the firm I loved. Coincidentally, I learned that Bill, who was now head of several departments within the company, wanted to hire a "deal guy" to travel to meet with developers. The job sounded so much more interesting to me than the one I had, so I asked Bill for an interview. He agreed. I did think it a little strange when he suggested we should meet over dinner in a restaurant. His explanation was that he didn't want my boss to find out that I was looking for another job. That sounded plausible to me.

After we had talked business for a while, we discussed other topics and some of my opinions about him began to change. He was sweet, interesting and likeable, but all I had on my mind was getting the new job. I found out later that he had no intention of offering me the job when he asked me to dinner. His sole purpose was to get to know me better, since I was about the only single woman in the company who showed absolutely no interest in him. Much later, he told me he had admired me from afar, but was reluctant to approach me, since he knew I was involved with someone else and also because he sensed I didn't approve of him. It was true.

During the course of dinner, he asked if I was going to attend the upcoming company Christmas dinner and dance with my boyfriend. I told him I was attending the dance alone since I was now without a boyfriend and that I was having a little cocktail party before the dance at my home. He mentioned he was also going to go to the dance alone and wanted to know if we should go together. I told him I already had made plans to go with my friend and her husband, but if he wanted to come to my party, he was welcome to do so.

He came to my party and stayed behind with me to help me clean up. We left together for the dinner and dance. After we arrived at the dance, the single women surrounded him and I danced my feet off with the other guys. Towards the end of the evening Bill saw me put on my coat to leave and he was at my side in a flash, asking where I was going. I told him I was going home, but he would have none of it. He ardently begged me to stay and talk and I relented. That night we shared a goodnight kiss and, to my complete amazement, I saw stars. He then asked me for a "real" date and I agreed.

Bill arrived for the first date at the same time an earthquake hit the area. He tells everyone that the earth moved under his feet on our first date! Four months later, we were married, which came as a shock to everyone.

June and Jack

as told by June.
Married in 1978 in Seacliff, Long Island, New York.
She was 53; he was 54. Jack died in 1994.

For Sale: After the Pool Party!

I was divorced in April and was being forced to sell what was our home. The home had a pool, and it was taking a while to sell. Now it was summer and I knew I would not have the pool again next year, so I decided to have a pool party. I invited a number of divorced and widowed women friends. To add to the fun, they each were required to bring an eligible male. I invited my neighbor who lived across the street whom I had once dated. One of my friends invited a guy named Jack who was in the process of getting a divorce.

Just before the party Jack called me and asked, "I got this crazy invitation. What is this about?" I explained and he said, "I guess I'll come." Everyone showed for the party, even a married guy. We all had a great time. I didn't see much of Jack at the party since he was in the house telling stories to a group of people. At the end of the party he was still there. We talked briefly and then he left.

Surprisingly, he called the next week and invited me for a date. I felt good being with him and felt we shared the same background. He was a businessman and a graduate of Cornell. I was a graduate of Duke. We both lived in the same area. He was a real sailor and loved to race Sunfish. I enjoyed watching him in his races. But he was not the only one in the picture. I had been invited to the Yacht Club to meet an attorney and ended up dating both men. I really was enamored with the attorney since he was well-to-do and had a great apartment in Manhattan. I enjoyed our time together walking all over the city, but I felt out of my element. I wanted to marry again and with someone I could feel more comfortable with.

During my time of dating both men, Jack kept asking me, "Are you my girl?" I would not answer. One day I told him that I broke off with the other guy. Soon after, he mentioned marriage and I jumped all over him. He was shocked and said he only wanted to think about it! Not too much later we announced our engagement to our families and married four months later at the Yacht Club. We were the only couple to marry from the pool party.

Peggy and David

as told by Peggy.
Married in 2004 in Roanoke, Virginia.
She was 38; he was 43.

Even Elvis Attended

We met online through a dating service, Match.com. I was very hesitant to go out with someone from a computer match. However, we met one afternoon at a local bar and hit it off. We wanted to get married right away but we were both still going through divorces. In due time, we found out that a local mall was offering to marry couples on Valentine's Day for free. We decided to get married at the mall. Since my other two weddings were really big and expensive and they didn't work out, I figured that I would try something different. A DJ performed the ceremony with approximately 20 other couples. The local news channels were there along with the local paper. Even Elvis was there! Afterwards, there was a free reception catered by a local restaurant.

We didn't tell too many people what we were doing, because we felt it was embarrassing. But by Monday the children at the school I worked at were asking me if that was me on the front page of the newspaper. Sure enough, it was me with my new husband.

About a month later my husband found out that his divorce was not final! We were upset but once we learned the divorce was finalized, we ended up going to a small town and getting married by a justice of the peace. But nobody knows about that ceremony. We still get kidded about our getting married at the mall with Elvis.

Priya and Rajesh

as told by Rajesh.
Married in 1981 in Mumbai, India.
She was 21; he was 28.

A Strategy for Life

I was living and working in the United States. Having been away for two years, I missed my family and friends in India and returned home for a long vacation.

Upon my arrival, my cousin and her husband visited me. We were chatting casually and they brought up the subject of marriage. They felt that I needed to be married. I communicated to them that *I* didn't feel the *need* to be married at this point in my life. However, my cousin's husband sold me on the idea of holding mutual interviews for the woman who would become my wife even though I was not looking for a wife! What I didn't know was that my cousin and her husband had already started the process and candidates were calling to have a date set for their interview.

At that time, it was very desirable for an Indian woman to meet a man living in the U.S who was educated and had a good job. Therefore, there were a number of friends, relatives, and acquaintances who wanted to be "prospective brides."

Typically the interviews are conducted with a group of family and friends of both the man and the woman. The meeting takes place, for example, at a restaurant or a friend's house. The groups consist of family and friends whose opinion the man and woman value. There are about 50 people who attend these meetings, which last one to two hours. This was very uncomfortable for me since the man must try to find some time away from the groups to talk with the prospective bride. Actually, I felt uneasy with all the friends and relatives interested in whom I would select and none of them wanted to be disappointed. The women also had the right to reject me, if they wish, while they are going through the interview process.

It is an anxious time for the women, too—so much so, that their relatives start calling the next day to see if a decision has been made yet. I was feeling a lot of pressure from both sides.

I decided to choose a few of the women to see again, one-on-one, as I felt I needed more time with some of them to be fair and make a decision. This didn't go over well, as that is not customary. In addition, the fact that I would ask to see a woman again in this manner meant more of a commitment to the woman's family, which could mean more disappointment. I persisted in what I wanted, though.

After I went through the second round of meetings, I conferred with my family and chose Priya to see again. Now I wanted to have her meet another cousin of mine, whose opinion mattered to me. The pressure continued for me to make a decision. I chose Priya and we went through an engagement ritual and then married. This whole process from meeting to marriage took 19 days! It seemed like a lifetime due to all the pressure.

After a honeymoon in Nepal, I returned to the U.S. by myself, and Priya returned to India. Priya needed all the proper paperwork to come to the U.S. Fortunately it only took a few months for all the details to be completed. She finally joined me to make a home in a country where she had never been before, with someone she didn't really know. We both adjusted and are happily married today.

Sheila and Lee

as told by Lee.
Married in 2001 in Atlanta, Georgia.
She was 47; he was 48.

Prayers Online

My previous wife had passed away after losing her four-year battle with cancer.

I had been getting emails from a Christian web site for quite a while. I liked the Bible studies and devotions. About a week after the funeral, I was online and noticed that the web site also had a way to meet other Christians. I decided to look into this.

One of the responses that I received had a picture of a beautiful woman in a glamour shot holding a clarinet. The caption read, "One shy of a duet."

We began to correspond and before I knew it, we had written 87 times in the first week and I was smitten! I didn't even know where she lived nor had I talked to her in person or on the phone. We figured that it was time to meet, so she invited me to Woodstock, Georgia to the Christmas presentation on Friday night followed by a single's church event the next night.

We agreed to meet at a restaurant in Woodstock. I called her to confirm our meeting and became weak-kneed just hearing her voice on the answering machine. Waiting at the restaurant, I anxiously watched for her and when I saw her—Wow! She was more beautiful than I imagined.

We went inside the restaurant and sat down and ordered. Before we ate, I took Sheila's hand and prayed that if this was the Lord's will for us to be together that we would know.

After we went to the Christmas concert, we went to the mall and stopped at a place for pictures.

Our photographer was not the sharpest tack in the box so it took a while to get us into the different poses. After one particular shot he left the room and came back with some mistletoe! After all it was Christmas time. I looked Sheila in the eye and said that I would be hanged if my first kiss were in front of this guy. So we gently kissed. We dated for the next several months and were married in June of the following year. Looking back, I was glad that we fell in love before we ever met. That made the physical part the icing on the cake rather than the foundation of our relationship and marriage.

Rose and Dennis

as told by Dennis.
Married in 1993 in Washington, D.C.
She was 25; he was 28.

In Search of Romance

I am very familiar with a movie titled, "90 days". It has to do with a guy wanting to marry a foreign bride. The bride-to-be travels to the U.S. and has 90 days to use as a trial period before her visa expires to see if she and the guy want to marry each other. I loved this idea. Based on my shy personality, I knew that approaching women or hanging out in a bar was not going to work for me. I decided to join a correspondence service and pay a fee to get pictures of women overseas who were interested in meeting an American guy to marry. The service put me in communication with a number of women from other cultures. I definitely had marriage in mind and continued with the service for about four years.

As I received the letters from the different women I began to get scared. The women all seemed to have the perception that the U.S. was the Garden of Eden. I wasn't quite sure they knew what they were getting into. I didn't want the responsibility if they were disappointed. So I changed my preference to be women who were living in the U.S.—preferably Filipino since they spoke English well.

Unforgettable: Vignettes of Love

One of the women I communicated with wrote to tell me that she thought she was too old for me. She suggested that I correspond with her niece and sent me the contact information. Her name was Rose. We wrote back and forth for about four months. I then took a bus to Northern Virginia to meet her. I proposed upon meeting her! When her sister found out we were to marry, she became upset because she wanted to marry, also. So, she arranged to marry the guy she was dating the same day we set for our wedding. We were married in a double ceremony.

Norma and Buck

as told by Norma.
Married in 1986 in Grand Prairie, Naval Air Station, Texas.
She was 31; he was 38.

It Was the Car!

We met through a fellow flight attendant of mine, Bonnie. Bonnie was flying a Delta flight from Dallas to LaGuardia. It was Easter Sunday and there were only five people on board. One of the passengers had taken what was normally the flight attendant's seat in the back of the plane. Bonnie thought that she would sit right next to the guy who took her seat and engage in conversation with him since she was not too busy. His name was Buck.

Before landing she told him that she had someone for him to meet so Buck gave Bonnie his card with his home number on it.

Bonnie gave me the card and shortly after I called him. I had to remind him of his talk with Bonnie. We then decided to get to know each other by phone for a month before meeting.

After that month, Buck invited me to Dallas, where he lived, to meet him. Fortunately my sister lived there, too, so I stayed with her. I found out later that Buck was freaked out about where to take me on this first date. He decided to take me to Six Flags, which was a good idea since I love roller coasters. However, I had just had a perm in my hair and now it was frizzy since the ride went through water. I also had wet clothes and was damp and embarrassed the rest of the day.

After cleaning up, I met Buck for dinner and asked him a lot of questions. I also told him that I wanted to marry and have children and was not just looking for sex. If he didn't want the same, don't call me. He was ready for me. Thank God since he was driving a red Maserati when we met and I thought, "This guy rocks!" I would have been disappointed if he did not call me even though he sold the Maserati the next day!

After our dinner date we continued to date with Buck commuting to Atlanta with his frequent flier miles to see me. I flew to Dallas as part of my job and visited him. After four months, I transferred to Dallas and moved in with Buck. We were married five months later.

# Alicia and Donald

as told by Alicia.
Married in 1997 in Newport Beach, California.
She was 57; he was 65.

How to Get a House in the Mountains

I was divorced and wanted to meet a companion and partner. I had tried a number of different avenues to meet a man. I went to dinner get-togethers and my friends tried to fix me up with their male friends. I told a friend I wanted to meet an older guy who liked to ski and had a house in the mountains. Nothing seemed to work.

I thought about moving back to Europe during this time since I was so lonely living in California. One day I received a voicemail from one of my friends. She called to invite me to the Hollywood Bowl. I accepted her invitation and agreed to meet her at her house to go to the Bowl. When I arrived, I met a guy named Donald.

I found out that Donald was a skier, owned his own shop and arranged ski and snowboard shows. I love the mountains and skiing and I thought what Donald did was interesting. Aside from all that, however, I thought he was just okay. We all went to the Bowl and after some wine and good food, I thought he looked better and better. But, I also felt that Don was very quiet and that he was probably intimidated with my being from Europe. Later that night, Don said he wanted to take me to dinner but was going with his mother on a cruise the next week. I suggested that we go to dinner the next day. He agreed.

We talked a lot at dinner and I felt he was caring and loving. Don had been left a widower and wanted to meet someone, too. I also felt that since he was taking his mother on a cruise, he was a good man. When Don left on his vacation, he sent me postcards every day. There were loving remarks on the cards. Once Don returned from his trip we dated every weekend.

Don mentioned that he had a place at Mammoth Mountain and told me how beautiful it was in the summertime. He asked me if I knew how to mountain bike and I said I did. So he agreed to take me to Mammoth. I had never ridden a bike in my life! I bought a bike and all the appropriate gear to look cool and impress him. He thought I must be a great biker when he came to pick me up seeing that I had this expensive bike and related clothes. Don took me to the top of the mountain in Mammoth. I told him to lead the way. I fell as soon as I started the ride. Don didn't see me fall but I was badly scratched and hurt. Don took me home and nursed me back to health. I explained to him that the bike was very different than what I was used to since it had 24 gears and was very complex. But then I confessed to him that I had never ridden a bike before. We gradually became interested in biking and even fishing and other activities and had a great time.

By Christmastime, I was ready to take Don to Poland to meet my son who lived there with his family. The trip proved memorable. Don became drunk since he was not used to the vodka. He also didn't like the food Polish people eat at Christmas and became very sick.

As is customary, we went to a big ball for New Years Eve that started at 10:00 p.m. and we danced until 5:30 a.m. Don could not walk the next day since he danced so much.

Looking for Mr. and Mrs. Right

We dated for one and a half years and then I asked him if he thought he was ready to marry. He hemmed and hawed. I suggested that we separate. I started dating others. Don tried to contact me several times over the next few weeks. He then visited me and I said I wanted a ring from him. He relented and we married on a yacht at sunset where guests came from Europe and Canada as well as the U.S., and we served Polish food. I fulfilled my wish of marrying an older man who liked to ski and had a house in the mountains!

Sang and Sun

as told by Sang.
Married in 1984 in Seoul, South Korea.
She was 26; he was 29.

Sent by God

I was a Sunday school teacher at my church. Sun was the leader of the youth group at the same church. When I first saw Sun, I thought he was very Christian and that God loved him very much. I was definitely interested in him. What I did not know until after we met was that Sun had been praying to God for a spouse for the last five years. Just in seeing me, he said to himself that I was the one for him and that God sent me to him and answered his prayers. Sun asked me out upon meeting me. He didn't have a job at the time except as the leader of the youth group. He was hesitant to meet my parents as parents in Korea wish to know that their daughters will be taken care of by the men they are intending to marry. However, my parents knew right away that Sun was a good man and a leader and had a lot of possibilities for employment. His parents loved me immediately. We dated for one year before we married. By that time Sun had obtained employment at a company he worked at many years before coming to the U.S.

Deborah and Peter

as told by Deborah.
Married in 1999 in South Burlington, Vermont.
She was 53; he was 42.

Out of Her Comfort Zone

I was 48 years old, and a single mom, for the second time. Life was good. We had just relocated to beautiful Vermont, and the kids were happy in school. I had been attending a local college, and had lots of good women friends, but something was missing. I had no one special to dine with or take in a movie—no special someone who noticed when I wasn't there, or when I was having a good day. I knew better than to expect "Mr. Right" to show up. But I thought I might find "Mr. Let's Do Dinner." But, how? Where?

I had been coaching myself for the next opportunity to meet

some people of the opposite sex who were old enough and available. I had a long talk with myself about making the effort and taking the risk. I was determined to accept that next invitation that came my way, and show up.

As it happened, the next invitation came to a party that fell on my birthday, which is in December. It was hosted by three women, one of whom was my neighbor. The location was a bit remote, a neighboring town I had never been to. I'm not good at finding my way in unfamiliar territory, but I was determined to take this opportunity to socialize. I was given directions by my friend and bought a good map just for the occasion. Then a snowstorm hit—a proper Nor'easter, a blizzard. It was the kind of night where activities were cancelled and the weather woman says, "If you don't absolutely have to go out, stay home!"

But I was determined. So I crept along and finally made it to my destination, the party.

Having arrived, the next phase of my mission was to mingle. I said to myself, "You're here, now get out there and converse like you have something to say!" I mingled my little heart out. It was a good evening, good music, food, and lots of conversation among those of us who braved it and made it to the party. I returned home in the deep snow, creeping along at 20 miles an hour, satisfied with myself for having made the effort.

The next day, I stopped by my neighbor's to say thank you. I told her what a good time I had. Among the people I talked about, I casually mentioned meeting a man named Peter. "He is such a nice guy," I said, "We talked about everything under the sun, sitting and grazing by the food table." I hadn't thought of him as someone I would date, because as we chatted, I learned he was 11 years younger than me.

I said good-bye to my neighbor, and as soon as I left she ran right to the phone to call Peter and tell him, "You need to ask this woman out! She likes you!" He did.

He called me at work and said, "Would you like to go out?"

I said, "You mean like on a date?" He said, "Yes."

We planned on dinner. I was a bit dubious at first, thinking he must have mixed me up with someone else (younger) from the party. He said, "No" and that he knew what he was doing. After he arrived to take me to dinner, we sat in my living room and talked non-stop for two hours. We finally remembered dinner and went to a restaurant that had just barely closed, but were serving dinner to the staff. They let us in and gave us a very romantic, very private dinner, and when he told me I was the most sensual woman he had ever met, I knew a little miracle had happened. We had found each other: the new Ms. & Mr. Right. We moved in together shortly after our dinner.

We were married in our garden at our home in Vermont and have been excruciatingly happy and building for a long future together.

Linda and Ed

as told by Ed.
Married in 1979 in Baltimore, Maryland.
They were both 23.

Mon Cher

I met my wife Linda in our freshman year of college. The dating scene was new to me up to this point. The only thing I remember about dating in high school was my mother telling me, "If you don't find someone to invite to your senior prom, I'll invite someone for you." I was very shy and most comfortable being a good student and sports enthusiast. My mother was concerned that I lacked interest in dating, and I was afraid she meant what she said about inviting someone to the prom for me. So, I asked a fellow classmate whom I barely knew and knew that I would never date her again.

I always knew that I would marry and wanted a family, I just wasn't quite sure how to get there. I felt that I was too inexperienced in the social scene to ask girls out. I figured that I would delay dating until I started college since I was not good enough to play collegiate sports, and would have more time to focus on dating that I did in high school. In my freshman year of college, I had a friend named Matt who was outgoing and knew a lot of people at our school. Matt was dating someone and committed to introduce me to people so we could double date. He had met a girl on campus he thought would be good for me. He said she was attractive, pleasant, smart and funny, all the characteristics I like. When he pointed her out to me one day, I recognized her from my French class. Her name was Linda.

I wanted to ask Linda out but was so shy that I found it difficult to speak directly to her. However, I knew that I could write notes to her, in French, of course, when we were in class. This way, I felt like I was still being conscientious to my studies and it would be safer than having to confront her face-to-face. We sent the notes through our mutual friend, Matt. He would read, edit and send them on. I would write to Linda asking her questions about herself, such as, what dorm she lived in, does she play sports (of course), all with the intent of getting to know her.

One of the exchanges of notes caught us all by surprise. We were writing notes about our families and during one exchange Linda shared that her mother had died when she was young and at that same time I had sent a note sharing that my father had died when I was young.

For some reason, this exchange of a very personal nature struck a chord in both of us. For our first date, we decided to double date with Matt and after that we never stopped. We both loved school so for a number of dates we found ourselves studying together and writing papers together. We dated all through college and once we graduated we discussed our future together and married two years later.

Margy and Frank

as told by Frank.
Married in 1982 in Winchester, Massachusetts.
Margy was 32; he was 33.

Your Brand Or Mine?

It was a late Friday night and I found myself in the local food store looking for dog biscuits. I overheard two women comparing biscuit brands. One of them asked if my dog liked the brand I was buying. I told her I didn't have a dog. They thought I was very weird, buying biscuits when I didn't own a dog. I explained I was a building contractor and I bought biscuits to give to clients' dogs when I was working on their houses. One of the women and I thought we knew each other from mutual friends so we all started talking.

About one and a half years earlier, I had lost my wife. I had two children from the marriage and was feeling very lonely. I wanted companionship, so I asked both women if they wanted to go for ice cream. They accepted. I enjoyed talking to both of them. One of them had a boyfriend, so I became interested in the other woman. Her name was Margy.

I suggested we go out again. Margy told me to give her a call the next week when she would know better. She apparently had some concerns. She knew I had two young children, which was a lot of responsibility, and she didn't trust I would really call her. I did and we went to a local diner and used the time to better introduce ourselves and learn more about each other. We talked for a very long time. She loved hearing about my children and loved seeing their pictures. She was an elementary school teacher and kids affected her. Unbeknownst to Margy, my older son had recently told me he wanted me to go out and find a new mother for him and his brother.

On our next date, I took Margy to an exclusive Boston restaurant for a great dinner. I then asked her to marry me. She was nervous and reminded me she hadn't even met the children. She wanted to see how our relationship developed over time and how the children responded to her. She still didn't believe I would keep calling her! I showed her. I kept calling.

When she met my children shortly after our dinner date, she bonded with them in no time. She began to care for them after school while I worked. On one of their first trips together, she took them to a pet shop and then to a veterinarian. The children loved it. I knew we were meant to be and was adamant that we marry.

I asked her mother for permission to marry Margy. Her mother surprised me by saying that I could have her daughter but never her pet dog or rabbit. Pets were beginning to play a big part in this relationship somehow! We were engaged the next Valentine's Day and married six months later. We went on to acquire a variety and number of pets from that day forward.

Michelle and Michael

as told by Michelle.
Married in 2005 in Prospect Harbor, Maine.
She was 37; he was 35.

Happy New Year!

It was New Years Eve and I had plans to go out with my friend Cynthia. We spent a little while at her apartment and then decided to stop by a bar called Rhone, located in the meatpacking district of New York City. We planned to have a drink and visit with Cynthia's friend who worked there. After getting a drink, all of a sudden we realized it was midnight and everyone was counting down. Since it's a tradition to kiss someone at midnight, Cynthia and I were talking about how we had no one to kiss and we needed to start the year out on the right foot. Cynthia grabbed the bartender and gave him a kiss. I said "What about me? Who can I kiss?" Cynthia walked up to a man standing at the bar and asked him if he was single. When he replied "Yes, why?," she said she wanted him to kiss her friend for New Year's. He looked over at me, and said, "OK" and we kissed. Then we introduced ourselves and spent the rest of the night talking. Two and a half years later we married.

chapter seven

The Female Pursuer

Patty and Fred

as told by Patty.
Married in 1959 in Leitchfield, Kentucky.
She was 18; he was 20. They divorced in 1974; Fred died in 1989.

The Cutest Girl in Town

I was the third generation to grow up in Leitchfield, Kentucky, which boasted a population of 12,000 in 1959.

My future husband Fred was from Chicago. He had just completed his two-year stint in the U.S. Marines and took a short detour to visit relatives in Leitchfield. While there, he asked his cousin to introduce him to the "cutest girl in town." Lucky me, Fred was deposited right at the front door of my family's timeless old two-story wood framed house on Main Street.

Fred looked like a movie star. His coal black hair, combed back in a slick ducktail framed a commandingly beautiful face. He took my breath away and I would love him forever.

Fred stayed at my house just long enough to pronounce, "If this is the cutest girl, this town is really hurting." After he left, I turned to my girlfriend who was standing by me and heard everything. Emphatically, I said to her, "I'm going to marry him." Her eyes became huge; she was speechless. I rushed by her and headed to the kitchen to tell my mother.

She listened and kept stirring the pot on the stove while I told her that I met the guy I was going to marry. She asked the name of his relatives in Leitchfield then she wiped her hands and went to the phone and called them.

Fred's aunt assured my mother that he came from a wonderful, reputable family. Once she hung up the phone, I hugged her and knew that she was supportive of me though concerned that I was so crazy over this guy.

The next day, I called Fred. I was confident, which was odd since I had received the biggest snub I'd ever had. Impulsively, I said, "You're going to take me to the movies tonight, aren't you?" He stammered and then gave a weak yes. That night we went to Leitchfield's only source of entertainment, the drive-in movie theater. As soon as we arrived, I asked him to put his arm around me. He slung his limp arm over my shoulders. I sat very still for a while and then I asked him to kiss me. His lips missed my cheek and landed on my ear. Then I said, "You're going to marry me, aren't you?" Wearily he said, "I guess so."

I was thrilled! Once he committed, I told him to take me home so I could tell my parents. When we arrived at my house, I jumped out of the car, saying I would let him know what day we were getting married. Then I rushed in and told my mother that I proposed and Fred said yes. He returned to his aunt and uncle's house and told them he was marrying me.

Soon after my mother put together an amazing church wedding for us with quite a crowd from Leitchfield in attendance. I think everyone in Leitchfield wanted to see the stranger from the big city who had swept me off my feet.

My future mother-in-law called before the wedding. She would not be able to attend but was looking forward to meeting me once we arrived in Chicago. Fred's younger sister then took the phone and told me Fred had a fan club in Chicago and that I would not be greeted warmly.

Right after the wedding and a one-night honeymoon in a motel, we drove on to Chicago where we lived during our marriage of 15 years. I went to work as a Playboy Bunny at the Chicago Club after my two children were born. One of Fred's "fan club" girls worked there and recognized me as the one who snared the-much-sought-after Fred from Chicago. I felt so superior when I met some of those swooning girls. They dismantled their fan club a month after we were married.

Jai and Vincent

as told by Jai.
Married in 2003 in Nonaburi, Thailand.
She was 23; he was 35.

Soul Mate Manifestation

I was living in Santa Monica, California and attended a seminar on how to attract what you want in life quickly. My roommate Alexis and her boyfriend, Conor, were at our apartment when I arrived home from the seminar. Conor worked at an educational enterprise that offers programs in effectiveness and communication for individuals. It was the same place where I took my seminar. I told them about a list I had created of what I wanted in a soul mate and I read it aloud to them. Conor said he had just the guy for me. His name was Vince. Conor worked with Vince and said to

The Female Pursuer

come by the office the next day to meet him.

I went to the office and I looked at Vince and walked out. Vince didn't see me do this and didn't know I was coming. All I saw was a guy with bad hair and an ugly brown suit. A few days later, Conor suggested that Vince and I talk by phone. We did and, although Vince knew by now that I had seen him and walked out, the conversation seemed to go well. We both knew that we couldn't date since employees of the enterprise could not date program participants.

A few days later I went back to the center for another program with my roommate Alexis. I saw this guy who I thought was very cute and asked Alexis who he was. Alexis said it was Vince. I was shocked and I said, "No, it can't be. This guy is cute!!"

A few weeks later I told my best friend that I had a crush on this guy named Vince. She told me to call him and I did. When he answered I said that I had something to tell him and stated sheepishly that I had a crush on him. He then told me that he saw me at one of the programs two years ago and thought to himself that I could be the one for him. Now two years later he saw me again and told Conor that he had to introduce us.

All of a sudden while we are still on the phone, he said he had to go. I was taken aback at him rushing off the phone. I didn't know it but his manager came in the office where Vince was talking on the phone. From there we would only see each other at the center until one day I asked him to a Halloween party. Even though Vince went to the party we decided to just remain friends since he wanted to be in integrity with his job and his personal life.

Our friendship continued. Even though things were not always rosy, we were each thinking all along that the other person might be the one for us.

One day Vince told me that he was going to spend a few months in India with his friend Conor. He planned on meeting with the Dalai Lama. I was going to be traveling to Thailand with my Thai mother at the same time, and I suggested that Vince meet me there. Vince quit his job so he could travel and now we could date! We finally had our first date. Vince kissed me on our way to my house after the date and from that point on, we spent every day together until he left for India.

We corresponded through email during our travels. Upon my arrival in Thailand, I asked my uncle if he would arrange for a blessing of Vince and Conor when they visited us in Thailand. My uncle is the type of person who goes all out and instead presented the idea of throwing a traditional Thai wedding for Vince and me. I messaged Vince to see what he had to say and he wrote back via email, "My little Thai wife. I like it." We were game. That night I looked at my original list of what I wanted in a soul mate. I put it away after seeing that Vince had all the qualities on my list.

Eight days later Vince and Conor arrived and we married in a beautiful Thai ceremony. We then traveled together for seven months before returning to Los Angeles.

Rebecca and Brian

as told by Brian.
Married in 1996 in Los Angeles, California.
She was 42; he was 39.

Romance Held Court

I was working as a criminal defense attorney who was trying a drunk driving case. Rebecca was working as a teacher and found herself selected to be on my jury. I wanted a teacher since I felt they are always fair or tend to favor the defense. She was also quite striking. She was elected the foreperson on the jury and, fortunately for my client and me, the jury came back with a not guilty verdict.

One month later, Rebecca called my office. She used the excuse that she wanted to leave teaching and wished to talk with me about being an attorney as a possible profession she could pursue. I found out later that her father and brother were attorneys so this was a ploy to connect with me.

I took her to lunch to talk and we hit it off quite well. We followed it up with another lunch about a week later at a little Chinese restaurant, which we both knew. During the conversation, Rebecca told me that she was on to my having a girlfriend since I took her to lunch and not dinner. I liked her instantaneously, as she was right. I told her that I was dating someone but it was going downhill, which was true. I asked Rebecca if I could call her and she agreed. We then began dating officially and decided to marry. We were married in the same courtroom where we met by the same judge who presided over the trial!

Joy and Ross

as told by Joy.
Married in 2002 in Philadelphia, Pennsylvania.
They were both 26.

Juggling Boyfriends

I started my professional career in a gutted warehouse stocked with makeshift cubicles as far as the eye could see. While embarking on a demanding career, I was also trying to manage my increasingly needy college boyfriend, Cooper, whom I lived with when I flew home from Harrisburg on the weekends.

I vaguely remember meeting Ross in those first few days. We literally sat across the aisle from each other so I checked him out as I collected things off the nearby printer.

In the coming months Ross approached me on one occasion to invite me to a project outing. I remember feeling like he was hitting on me, so to deter any flirtation, I said, in a bitchy tone, "Well, if I came out, I would want to drink and, since I have no plans on hooking up with any of you, then how would I get a ride home?" With that, he looked at me like I was crazy and walked away.

That night I started thinking about how mean I had been. The next day, I took a deep breath and walked over to Ross's desk and apologized. He forgave me and from there, a friendship blossomed. I convinced myself this was innocent and I wasn't attracted to Ross but my heart was telling me otherwise. I started to say hello or flash my most charming smile every time I went to the printer.

I had always "chain-smoked" boyfriends, starting a new relationship before ending the existing one. I continued to hang out with Cooper on the weekends and carry on this friendship with Ross during the week. Soon, I found myself thinking of Ross all the time. One evening, Ross came over to hang out, and I had a heart-wrenching conversation with him about my state of mind and how unhappy I was with Cooper and how guilty I felt about it. He just listened and hugged me tight before he left. That hug changed everything.

I invited Ross over the following Thursday under the guise of watching the last episode of "Seinfeld" together and he accepted. Ross was receptive to my moves that night. I must admit I don't remember many of them but waking up in his arms the next morning felt natural and worth every risk I was taking.

We spent the next two months falling in love. We clicked on every level and for some unknown reason, Ross never judged me. He never demanded I end things with Cooper or became frustrated over my inability to decide between the two of them. He simply took things one day at a time and enjoyed every moment. He was amazing.

My assignment in Harrisburg ended. I had moved out of Cooper's, but he had no clue that I had fallen in love with someone else. I found myself becoming increasingly depressed at the realization that I was the type of person that could betray someone that trusted me. I was ashamed that even my best girl friend had no idea that I was in love with a mystery man from work. Within weeks of leaving Harrisburg, I was assigned to a project in PA, only one hour from Ross. That was it for me. We reunited, and with a few bumps in the road, built the foundation that our marriage stands on today.

Pam and Paul

as told by Pam.
Married in 2004 in Harrington, Delaware.
She was 44; he was 38.

Once Upon A Time

A fairytale is a fictitious, highly fanciful story. Our story of how we met is very true and very real even though it culminated in a fairy tale happening.

My last name is "Galyean," and I was married to a wonderful man named Dan Galyean before he died in 1996. I have a daughter and a son. In 1999, my son finally talked me into buying a computer and stepping into the 20th century. When I set up my email account, under the name of 'pgalyean', I was told the name was already being used. I thought to myself, "Now how many 'pgalyean's can there be in the world?"

I wrote to this person, asking who he was and if we could be related in some way. The person who wrote back was named Paul Galyean, and he lived in Arizona. We sent emails back and forth for a few months, finding out about each other and trying to figure out if he was somehow related to my late husband's family.

As it turns out, Paul's stepfather adopted him when he was 18, and Paul took his last name, "Galyean." Paul told me he had three children and was separated. We not only had the same last name given to us by special men, but we each had a son with the same name, Michael. Too weird.

We sent emails to each other every now and then after I had to change my email address since Paul had 'taken' mine. We lost touch for about a year when I heard from him in a strange way.

When I set up my Yahoo account in February 2001, there was a name I didn't recognize in my friend's list. When I instant messaged this person, I learned it was Paul again, using a nickname from school. I learned Paul had moved back to his hometown of Dallas, Texas and was now divorced. We started chatting and I learned that his stepdaughter had recently passed away. I was writing a term paper for my psychology class about the stages of grief, and I was able to offer my help to him and his youngest daughter. Having experienced grief myself, I was able to tell him and his daughter what emotions to expect. We formed a very close bond through this experience.

We began to send each other emails every day, and we chatted almost every night on the computer and occasionally on the phone. Finally, after three months of talking every day, I decided to take the next step. I asked Paul if it would be okay for me to come to Texas to meet him. He said of course. I knew I was taking a lot of chances. Some might have thought this a stupid idea, but something told me that I needed to do this; that this guy was special.

I arrived in Texas in June of 2001, and I met the man that I was already falling in love with. We had a great time getting to know each other. When I had to leave, it was heartbreaking. I knew it would be a long time before I was able to see Paul again. I had lost my husband, and now I felt that I was losing Paul.

After I returned home, we continued to talk. It was hard hearing his voice and not being with him. Paul called me one night in late June asking if I wanted to be with him forever. He was willing to leave his job and his home and move to Delaware to be with me. I couldn't believe he was willing to do that for us. He moved here in July 2001 and we were engaged on Valentine's Day of 2002.

We planned on marrying and had heard of a contest being run by the Delaware State Fair. It asked couples to submit a unique "fairytale story" to win a fairytale-style wedding. We entered the contest. The day of the winning announcement came and we dressed hoping that someone would be at our door between the allotted hours. No one showed, so we figured we lost, changed into grungy clothes and started doing household chores. While changing the toilet in the bathroom we heard the doorbell ring. We opened the door and were shocked to see a TV crew standing there to surprise us with balloons and an envelope with the appropriate paperwork to give us a fairytale wedding! We were thrilled!

On our wedding day the groom and wedding party were escorted in horse-drawn carriages, and my father and I arrived in a horse-drawn pumpkin carriage—just like Cinderella! We were married on the fairgrounds, during one of the largest events in Delaware with everyone celebrating with us.

chapter eight

It Happens

Johnita and Lionel

as told by Johnita.
Married in 1968 in Oklahoma City, Oklahoma.
She was 25; he was 35.

1 + 1 = 8

I was living in a small town in Oklahoma and dating a dentist. He told me he was separated from his wife and they were to be divorced. One day I received a call from his wife and she told me they were not separated and she wished to keep the marriage intact. She asked to meet with me to talk about my dating her husband. I agreed and I realized that I liked her as a friend. I told her that I would stop dating her husband. I didn't see him anymore even though he kept calling me. She contacted me again shortly after and asked to get together and told me that I was not the only woman her husband was dating. We decided to get together with all of the women who had been or continued to be with her husband and invite all of them to lunch. Everyone showed up and we had a good time!

Shortly after the lunch I decided to move to Oklahoma City. The dentist's wife found out and asked if she could move with me and be my roommate. Her marriage with the dentist was ending since she realized it was too difficult to make it work. So we moved in together. Each of us has a daughter and we brought them along. After a period of time, she moved out on her own with her daughter and started dating again. She met a man who had a friend by the name of Lionel. She asked me if I would like to meet Lionel since he was a divorced father of five. I asked her why I would want to get involved with anyone with five children! I was not interested in getting serious with anyone, especially someone with all those children. I did agree to get together with all of them though just for the evening.

When we arrived at Lionel's house, all I saw were all of these children running out of the house. I was beside myself and was not happy and I showed it. Lionel told me to lighten up and come join everyone in the house. Fortunately, we had a fun evening. I didn't realize until I arrived home that I left my reading glasses on the back of the sofa. I went back to get them the next day. Lionel and I ended up spending a lot of time talking that night and into the wee hours of the morning. Lionel was a lot of fun. That was on July 12.

We married one month later on August 12. I realized in the month between that Lionel was the most mature, stable, calm, confident man I had ever dated. He handled his five children with such ease. They played chess; they did word games at the dinner table. Nothing ever upset him. I was so impressed.

We started our marriage with six children between us. We rushed into marriage since my stepfather had leukemia and we wanted him to be at our wedding. We knew he would not make it if we waited longer. My mother had to leave town to be with my stepfather in the hospital so the responsibility to care for my three stepbrothers fell on me temporarily. We came home from our one-night honeymoon to nine children.

Emma and Joe

as told by Emma.
Married in 1945 in Stafford, England.
She was 19; he was 23.

It's The Gift That Counts

We both lived on our respective military bases in England. Joe was a Corporal in the U.S. 8th Air Force stationed in Sudsberry, England and I was a private in the Royal Air Force in Stafford, England. We met by chance in the town of Stafford one evening. I was walking down the street with my girlfriend. Joe was walking with a buddy and they said "hi" to us. The men asked if they could walk us back to our base and they did. Joe made a date with me for the next night. Our friends didn't connect that night, but we did.

We started dating. However, I was very popular and was dating several others. About the fourth date with Joe, I thought of telling him that I no longer was interested in dating him. But that was the night that he brought me a special gift—a pigskin leather compact. That was such an unusual and expensive gift that I decided to continue dating him! About eight weeks later Joe proposed to me and I accepted.

I was using the name "Emmy" as I thought Emma was so old fashioned. In fact, it was also my mother's name and now is a very popular girl's name (# 1 in 2005). Joe made out the marriage license paperwork with the name Emmy and it had to be corrected once I acknowledged my true name. I was also surprised later to learn his middle name was Peter. All I had seen was Joseph P.

In June of 1946 Joe was shipped back to the U.S. I arrived in America in August of that same year. We remained in the U.S. and raised our five children.

Kathy and Tom

as told by Kathy.
Married in 1982 in Fort Wayne, Indiana.
She was 25; he was 24.

We Did It Our Way

My mother and father worked on the building of a church with others in the community. Once the church was completed, I taught Sunday school and managed some of the church operations. Members of the congregation thought I should marry someone who is a minister due to my being so active in the church. In the past, I had been fixed up with two seminary students from a nearby seminary school who I was repulsed by and was not interested in meeting anyone else.

A class was to be taught for the local Sunday school teachers and Tom, a seminary student, was assigned to teach a particular lesson. After he completed his section, he called a break for the class but stayed for the remainder of the day. During the break the seating arrangement was reconfigured. When I returned to the class, there were only two seats available, which were next to each other. Tom took one and I was forced to take the other and sit next to him. Tom didn't know that the pastor and other parishioners wanted to get us together. I was mortified knowing they probably arranged all of this.

Once the class was over, it was my responsibility to lock up the church and Tom remained to ensure all went well. We met in the parking lot and started talking. Tom asked me to go for coffee. I felt the urgent need to go home since I really had to go to the bathroom, so I hurriedly asked him to my apartment the next night for dinner. I also asked him if he had any allergies and he said yes he was allergic to nuts.

That same week our town had a flood and the streets were still filled with water. I had temporarily moved to my parents for a few days since the street where I lived was hit badly. I was back at my apartment and when Tom arrived he had to remove his shoes and socks and roll up his pant legs to get inside. We had dinner but I had forgotten about his allergies. I served several dishes that had nuts in them. He ate the food since he wanted to be polite. Shortly after he ate dinner he rushed from the apartment and went home to take Benadryl!

After several weeks when he was sure I was not trying to kill him, he called and asked me out. I was surprised that I enjoyed being with him. He was a relaxed guy, happy with life and, consequently, a lot of fun. He also enjoyed being with me. We dated quietly for a few months until we arrived at a church potluck dinner together. Now the congregation knew we were dating.

Tom invited me to his hometown two months later, in Wyoming to meet his parents. Tom wanted to be sure I could accept his brash father before he proposed. His father did surprise me with some of his off-color statements, but I managed. Tom proposed upon his return to Indiana. Since we didn't know where Tom would be assigned and didn't want to be apart, we felt the need to rush and married eight weeks later. The whole congregation was invited to the wedding. We found out later that they thought we rushed the wedding because I was pregnant.

Kay and Richard

as told by Richard.
Married in 2005 in Kona, Hawaii.
She was 33; he was 56.

Against All Odds

Kay was working in a food court at the department store in Phuket, Thailand. Kay is Thai and was working there serving local food. I was a tourist from the United States and had also been living in Thailand for approximately nine months before I began going to the food court. I went there many times. Each time I went, we would make conversation even though Kay couldn't speak English and I couldn't speak Thai. I would sometimes bring friends to help translate and aid in the conversation.

I could tell there was something special about Kay. I had been with several other Thai ladies but I felt that every one wanted something from me, but Kay never asked for anything. Kay already had married once before and was divorced with a six-year-old son. Kay would work twelve hours including overtime from 9 a.m. to 9 p.m. I would come to the food court at various times and I could always tell that she looked forward to seeing me. Kay was falling in love with me. After about three months, I asked Kay to stay with me. She thought about it and felt it would be okay. She always felt secure and protected by me.

For the next five years we lived in Thailand and used a translation device to communicate. After five years, I wanted to move to the Big Island in Hawaii. In order for me to bring Kay with me, we had to marry. I know that no one has ever loved me like Kay does.

Mary Ann and Ray

as told by Mary Ann.
Married in 1973 in Springfield, Massachusetts.
She was 25; he was 32.

Cape Cod Romance

The summer of 1973 is the summer I met my husband, Ray.

I was 25 and vacationing for the weekend with my younger sister, Donna. We were staying with three male friends of hers whom I had just met. We went out to dinner in Hyannis at the very crowded "Velvet Hammer." The only places left to sit were at the bar, which we did. One of the guys went to see a friend at one of the other tables.

The bar was dimly lit and smoky and when a guy asked if he could sit on the empty seat next to me, I made room for him, thinking he was the guy from our group who left a few minutes before. As soon as he sat down, I realized that he was a stranger. However, we began talking about beaches on the Cape. He said he spent the day at Craigsville Beach. He continued on, telling me that his name was Ray and how he had ridden his motorcycle down from Boston; and, as one did in the 70's, how he was a Leo and that was why he was so friendly.

We were having such a good time; I didn't tell him I initially thought he was someone else. We both enjoyed each other's company while we ate our steak dinners. My sister and her friends were busy eating and talking to some other people they knew, so when Ray asked if I wanted to go for a ride on his motorcycle, I said sure. I recently ended a long-term relationship and was looking for some fun and adventure. I told my sister I was leaving and would see her back at the cottage. Little did I know it would be the next morning.

We rode his motorcycle along windy Cape Cod roads, and then we picnicked on wine, pretzels and cheese at Coast Beach until dawn. After he dropped me off, I thought I'd never see him again.

Since I was a Leo, too, I remembered his birthday was the following week. His name and address were listed in the phone book, but when I called to see if he received the card I sent, his Dad, Ray Sr., answered the phone instead! He gave me Ray's correct phone number, and that started the frequent phone calls that turned into frequent weekend visits. He would take the train to Norwalk, Connecticut where I lived and worked, and the next weekend I would take the train to Boston to see him.

What I did not know until a few weeks into the relationship was that Ray was divorced with three children. He was reluctant to tell me, thinking I would not have anything to do with him, similar to the other women he had met and dated. However, being a teacher,

I loved children and we all hit it off when we finally met. This was important to Ray as to whether to continue with the relationship.

By October, I had met his parents and he had met mine. On November 2nd, he proposed over the phone and I said, "Yes!" We both wanted to marry and felt we were ready. The next weekend, I drove up to Boston. He met me at the bottom of the back stairs to his second floor apartment. A ring was waiting at the top of the staircase, which I found after picking up the red rose that awaited me on each step leading up to it. Seven weeks later we were married.

Kathryn and Alfred

as told by Kathryn.
Married in 1935 in Washington, D.C.
She was 25; he was 24. Alfred died in 2000.

Songbird of the South?

Alfred moved to Pennsylvania from England with his family. My sister commuted with Alfred to college in Pittsburgh. One day she brought him home and introduced him to me. My sister thought he would be good for me. I thought nothing of it. Alfred continued to stop by since he was attracted to me. I was dating a few other guys and it took a while for me to know that I had feelings for him. He asked me to go steady and then I decided to only date him.

Alfred had a beautiful tenor voice and would often sing to me. He entered a contest in Pittsburgh and won. I was impressed and proud of him. We dated for about four and a half years before marrying. Our courtship was during the Depression. Not having much money, Alfred went without lunch for months to buy me an engagement ring.

Alfred was a naval architect and was transferred to South Carolina for his job six months before we were to marry. We wrote each other every day.

Since he didn't have much time off from his job we planned to travel to Washington, D.C. to get married since that was about half the distance between where we were each living and would save time. I was scared when my wedding day approached. I had not seen him in six months. I kept thinking am I doing the right thing? But when I saw him I knew this was it. I knew that I wanted him. We moved to South Carolina after the wedding. Alfred continued to sing and was hired to sing on the radio in Charleston. He became known as the "Songbird of the South," even though we were really from the North!

Detric and Charlie

as told by Detric.
Married in 1998 in Lithonia, Georgia.
She was 39; he was 71.

Throwing His Hat in the Ring

I had been going to the same restaurant every day for breakfast or lunch for two years. Almost every day I would see many of the same people who also frequented the restaurant but I didn't know them. Charlie would say, "Hello," or "Good morning," to me but that was the extent of our conversation.

One Friday Charlie passed by while I was eating my lunch. He stopped and placed five $1 bills next to my plate and told me to pay for my lunch with the money. He then left the restaurant. When I returned on Monday one of the workers at the restaurant approached me and gave me Charlie's business card and said to call him. I called him and thanked him for the lunch from the previous Friday. Charlie told me that the manager at the restaurant had told Charlie to "put his hat in the ring as there were a lot of people watching me." I had been asked out by a few patrons of the restaurant but had never accepted their invitation. Charlie, however, felt now that he needed to throw his hat in the ring. He asked me out for dinner a few days later and I accepted.

    Charlie owned a vacant home he had been fixing up to rent. After our first date, he asked me to meet him at this house. He had a small table and chairs in the kitchen with a black and white TV. I would join him every day after work to have a snack. Charlie knew that I liked Martell cognac and he would have it waiting for me each day. Once Charlie's house became rented, he and I would meet at my house. I was able to purchase a house and Charlie helped me fix it up. We dated for three years and then married.

Maria and Tony

as told by their daughter.
Married in 1937 in Reno, Nevada.
She was 19; he was 27. Maria and Tony are both deceased.

It Was in the Cards

Maria and Tony met near French Camp, California. Tony was quite the dashing figure with his Model A Ford and had the nickname of "Frenchie," since his parents came to the U.S. from France. Tony was a farmer. Maria was a first-generation, Portuguese woman, working as a "nanny" for the son of a prominent ranch couple. When sheep-shearing season arrived in the spring, Tony helped with shearing, like everyone who lived in small farm communities. He spied Maria down by the pens with the children she cared for. Interested, he asked the rancher who she was and where he might meet her.

Entertainment in the area consisted of street whist (card) parties and Portuguese dances. Tony started showing up at every card party and Portuguese celebration event in the area, until finally one night he saw Maria at a whist party. Hoping to impress her, he played recklessly and won big. She noticed and asked someone to introduce Tony to her. After meeting, they started dating and they eloped that fall. Maria's younger sister met her husband at the same ranch where Tony and Maria met.

Britta and Manfred

as told by Britta.
Married in 1994 in Groemitz, Germany.
She was 30; he was 44.

Never Dating Again

I had just gone through a breakup in a relationship that I had had for four years and was sitting in a café in my hometown. I had decided never to date again. Manfred had just experienced a breakup in a relationship with his girlfriend of seven years and was very upset.

Manfred found himself doing his laundry at a laundromat and waiting for it to dry. While waiting, he decided to stop in the café next door. When he walked in, he felt drawn to sit with me. He didn't know me, but said that he felt it necessary to sit at the same table even though there were empty seats elsewhere. I was intrigued that Manfred was wearing a baseball cap and had a great tan. We started talking and he explained that he just returned from a vacation in Florida. I was very impressed that here was someone who had just traveled to the U.S., where I had only dreamed of visiting. I was enjoying our conversation. Before Manfred returned to the laundromat next door, he wanted to know if he would continue to see me. He suggested that I meet him the following weekend at the "strandkoerbe" that he had rented for the season by the coast.

(The strandkoerbe is a large wicker beach chair that sits two people and has a canopy top and foot rests attached to the base. It is private and romantic and protects people from the wind and the sun.) I was apprehensive to wear a bathing suit on our first date but I went ahead with it anyway. We both had a great time and saw each other every day after that.

When I introduced Manfred to my mother, she noticed the baseball cap he was wearing and thought it was strange. It was unusual for people in our town to wear such a cap. My mother pulled me aside and told me to tell Manfred to remove the cap. Manfred went along with it and all went well with the relationship and my family. He and I married close to one year after dating.

Jeri and Michael

as told by Michael.
Married in 1996 in Evergreen, Colorado.
They were both 44.

The Matchmaker

I was living in Colorado. I went on a business trip to Miami, where I used to live. My sister, who lives in Coconut Grove, took me to the Coconut Grove art show. As we were walking around the show my sister bumped into a woman she knew from her ballet class. I was introduced to her and her husband. We all went our separate ways. However, the woman from the ballet class later told my sister that she thought I would be perfect for her husband's ex-wife, whose name is Jeri. She and Jeri have a good relationship and all involved were very friendly with each other.

The wife tried to get us together and gave me Jeri's phone number in Miami. Neither one of us was very interested in a blind date, but she kept trying to convince us that it would be a good idea. It took about a year, but I finally reached Jeri by phone shortly before another trip to Miami. She seemed uninterested, which surprised me because I had been told she really wanted to meet me, but she agreed to get together.

At our first meeting, I brought my best friend and his wife in case it didn't work out well. We went to a French restaurant. I thought

Jeri was nice, but nothing special. She felt the same, but we both still wanted to get to know each other. We went out several times during the week I was in Miami. The last night together we went dancing. Jeri later said that was when she could feel herself falling in love with me. For me, it happened more gradually.

I returned to Colorado and kept thinking of her. We kept in touch, and then two months later I invited her to go camping along with my children who were with me for the summer. She stayed for a week. Two months after that, I asked her to move to Colorado. She did, and we eventually married. Once the dust settled and we were comfortable with each other, Jeri told me she remembered talking with a friend who was a psychic years before we even met. The psychic asked her, "Do you want to know about your soul mate?" Jeri did, and the psychic said her soul mate's name is Mike. To make it more unbelievable, she described how I looked!

Lupe and Paco

as told by Paco.
Married in 1997 in Granada, Spain.
She was 27; he was 29.

Going it Alone

Lupe and I were each living in Granada at that time. I was in my fourth year at the university and she was living at home with her family and attending the same university. After so much time in Granada, I was eager to go skiing even though I had little experience with the sport. A friend of mine and I went to the University of Granada to gather some information about the different ski courses they offered. There was one at the beginning of April that would fit in well with our academic schedule and we decided to sign up for the course. Days before the course my friend told me he wasn't going to do it. I had made my decision and decided to go for it.

This is exactly what happened to Lupe. She had always wanted to try to learn how to ski but, for some reason, had never had the chance to do it. One day she and a group of her friends received information for a beginner ski course, starting in April. For some unexpected reason, all her friends had some sort of problem that didn't allow them to take the lessons that week. In spite of that, she decided to take the course.

So, here we were, two complete strangers, with a bunch of other students like us on our way to the Sierra Nevada for our first ski lessons. I had been there two or three times before and had even purchased a pair of skis, a pair of boots, and some accessories like gloves and sunglasses. For the first minutes on the snow all of us were together trying to put on our pair of skis. When I was finished, I saw there were many people in the group who had never stood on a pair of skis. And then I looked around to see there was a nice girl right beside me who could not even stand by herself without repeatedly falling. I thought, "How can I not help her?" This was my first contact with Lupe.

After a couple of minutes, the teachers came and we were divided into groups according to our level. She was placed in the beginners group and I was in the next one. This meant that we might not see each other during the four days we were doing the course. But, then, on the last day, a group of us thought it would be a good idea to meet with the rest of the people from the first day.

A group of ten to fifteen people met to have a drink and dance in the city. It was on that night when Lupe and I started to talk a little bit more. That was the moment when I started to be more interested in her. We were dancing and her friends were leaving. I told her that I could take her home so that she didn't have to leave so early and she agreed. When I took her home I asked her if we could meet the next day. She answered, "Why not?" As I found out later, when I asked her to come out with me she thought it was going to be the whole group, not just the two of us. Fortunately, she had a good time.

After we dated for some time, I asked her to marry me and she accepted. We married on Lupe's birthday at the Cathedral of Granada.

Gracia and Al

as told by Gracia.
Married in 1971 in Willow City, North Dakota.
They were both 23. They divorced in 1982.

So Many Men...

Following graduation from nursing, I accepted a commission as an Ensign in the Navy and received orders to go to the Great Lakes Naval Hospital (GLNH) north of Chicago. I became assigned as a charge nurse in the Intensive Care Unit (ICU) where servicemen injured in Vietnam were treated. Traditionally, enlistees and officers didn't socialize in the military but it was different in the medical corps. We all worked very closely as a team.

When Al came home from Vietnam, he was assigned as a medic to the ICU at GLNH. The women in my unit, as well as myself, found him very handsome and appealing. After our shifts, the staff would frequent a local bar named "Poor Neal's." The senior corpsman in ICU, Kenny, had an off base job as a bartender. He asked me to the bar one evening but was bartending, so he needed to work behind the bar most of the night. We would try to chat between his filling orders.

When Al arrived, he sat next to me at the bar, not knowing that Kenny and I were on a date. Al started flirting with me and making suggestive comments. I was enjoying the attention. When the rest of the medical team arrived at the bar, Al and I moved to be with them at a large table. While we were sitting at the table, Al reached for my hand under the table and we sat holding hands. Kenny came over during one of his breaks and sat on the other side of me. He took my other hand. Now I was sitting at the table with a different guy on each side of me, each holding one of my hands! What is a girl to do? Well, I was really falling for Al. He asked me out and I accepted.

The day arrived for our first date. I was waiting for him to pick me up. The time was clicking away and there was no sign of Al. I figured he was doing this deliberately and that he was dumping me. He, however, was lost and getting very upset at being lost. He thought I had purposely given him a wrong address. When he finally arrived, an hour late, we were both mad at each other. What a way to start dating! We dated 10 months before getting engaged and then married the following year.

Paulette and Henry

as told by their granddaughter.
Married in 1928 in Bergen County, New Jersey.
She was 22; he was 24. Paulette and Henry are both deceased.

Ma Bell Connecting Mr. Right

Paulette was one of 13 children and just a child when her father passed away. After a few years and to make ends meet, Paulette's mother accepted and operated the very first telephone switchboard for Bergen County, New Jersey. Since all the daughters were also employed as operators, they converted the family dining room into the call center. Paulette's mom felt that her children didn't need many outside activities, with all the sisters being so close in age so Paulette didn't get out much. There was, however, the telephone.

Henry grew to recognize Paulette's voice whenever he made a call and she was the one to connect him. This was the type of system where you couldn't make a call directly; you used an operator, just like on "The Andy Griffith Show". It was strictly against the rules to chat with any customer and a bit difficult with her sisters sitting on either side of her. On overnight shifts, however, when the other sisters were asleep, Paulette and Henry learned more about each other. Initially there was little chance of any real romance developing because Henry was Catholic and Paulette was Methodist. Dating a person of a different religion was still considered taboo in the early

1900's. Over time, they finally agreed to meet anyway and somehow the differences in their faiths became insignificant to them and they decided to marry.

A small civil ceremony was performed with just two witnesses. The couple couldn't make a big deal out of the wedding due to their different religions. In fact Paulette was sure the ceremony was the rehearsal until the Justice of the Peace assured her that they were really married. Paulette and Henry lived and died happily ever after thanks to our friends at Bell Telephone.

Betsy and Dean

as told by their granddaughter.
Married in 1945 in Flint, Michigan.
She was 30; he was 29.

What's in a Name?

Betsy was already divorced. She went to a bar one night where she had met a soldier and had a great time. The next night she returned to the same bar and ran into Dean, who was also a soldier. She was afraid Dean might know her date from the previous evening so she told him her name was "Betsy." She hit it off with this soldier, too. He was soon transferred but he and Betsy wrote back and forth. When he returned, they married. She continued to go by Betsy and never told Dean that Betsy was not her real name! In time, he did find out from others but never knew why she made up the name.

Rachel and Henry

as told by Henry's sister.
Married in 1982 in Dodge City, Kansas.
She was 20; he was 24.

Little Sister's Little Friend

My brother Henry is very intelligent and was into being a hippy in early 1981. He was attending Washburn University School of Law at Topeka and I was attending Brown Mackie College in Salina. It was the Thanksgiving holiday break. He was riding home with me from Salina to our hometown of Dodge City because we were afraid his car wouldn't make it. All the way home he kept pestering me to "fix me up with one of your little friends." My brother is five years older than me so he really didn't know any of my friends.

After getting back to Dodge, my best friend came over to my house and we were talking about him and his needing a "fix up." I decided I didn't want to ever do this again so, I thought if I fixed him up with someone he hated, he would never ask me to fix him up again and leave me alone.

My brother *really* didn't like "ditzy" women. So we sat and thought about the ditziest girl we knew. We had a high school friend named Rachel who was really sweet and kind, very involved in school, and very ditzy. She would be perfect! He would think she was too ditzy, have a horrible time and never ask me to fix him up again. So we called Rachel and she agreed to be fixed up with my brother. She would meet us at a local club that evening so she could meet him.

When we were at the club later that day it was very crowded. My brother and I had to share a chair. Rachel came in and said "hi," but didn't really look too interested. After a while, I went over to talk to her and asked what she thought of him. She thought he was my date since we were sharing a chair, so she really hadn't paid that much attention to him. She said, "I guess he's kind of cute." I didn't know if she really meant it or didn't want to hurt my feelings, but at least she was game to go on with the blind date.

I went back to the table and told Henry to go ask her to dance. They went out on the really loud dance floor for a song or two and then he came back and sat back down with me. I asked him how it was going. He said, "I guess she's alright, but she's a little weird." I told him he needed to keep trying.

They went out and danced some more. Then, they were sitting together at our table. I thought, "They're making progress." I went off and danced and talked to other people. It was getting late and the place was about to close, so I started looking around for them. I found out later my brother wanted to go home with Rachel but she refused. My brother and I went back to our house.

On the trip back to college I asked if he liked Rachel. He said she was "Ok" and maybe he would call her. I thought that meant he wanted to give her the brush off and that he really didn't like the fix up, and I was safe and would never have to "set him up" again.

Rachel and Henry didn't see each other again until Christmas. Rachel came to our parents' house to go out to dinner with me and other friends. Henry asked if he could come along. They were both attracted to each other when they met initially and were now acting on the attraction. During the Christmas vacation, Rachel and Henry saw each other every night. He even left his watch at her house and realized it when he returned to college. When she called him to let him know that she had it, he suggested that she hand deliver it to him. She took a train to see him on several occasions over the next few months.

I was right about never having to set him up again. They were engaged by March and married by summer. They have been happily married with two children and a myriad of foster children sharing their lives.

Susan and Bob

as told by Susan.
Married in 1981 in Atlanta, Georgia.
She was 42; he was 46.

Divine Intervention

I had left Detroit on my way to New Hampshire and the plane made a stop in Cleveland, Ohio. A man sat down next to me and I noticed that the flight attendants knew him and brought him a drink prior to take off. He asked me if I might like one too, and I accepted. He proceeded to shuffle through papers in his briefcase and obviously saw himself as very important and busy. I was reading and as the flight proceeded he started a conversation and introduced himself as Bob. Then we told each other about ourselves.

As the plane landed he casually mentioned that he often came to Detroit and asked me if I would have lunch with him. I told him that I didn't have lunch with men I met on airplanes and left the plane to meet a girlfriend who I was spending the weekend with.

On Monday morning I boarded the plane and made my way to my seat. I had to climb over an already seated passenger. It happened to be Bob from Friday night! He looked up and smiled and said "Hi, can I buy you breakfast?" Whether it was fate or divine intervention we will never know but that was the beginning of a friendship that resulted several years later in marriage.

The End

Acknowledgments

This type of book is only possible through the efforts of many people. I only hope that I do not fail to remember all who assisted me with this book, whether it was in boosting my confidence or giving me a "juicy" story. I wish to thank each storyteller in the book who willingly shared their special memories knowing how they can inspire, delight and warm the hearts of all of us.

I would also like to thank those friends and family who supported me during this project while communicating their interest in the book. I first interviewed my long-time friend Pat Colonna, who recited his story to me, and then received the next via email from my cousin Pam Rossi. Friends like Beth Gelb took on a personal campaign to get stories for me from her friends. I was on my way! I then hit the road and traveled to pockets of states explaining what I was looking for to everyone I met.

Thank you to my cousin Phyllis Squillante for listening to the stories as I was collecting them on the road and to Debbie Bennett and Sarah Densmore who I recounted them to when I returned home, along with Sylvia Kaye and Brooke Philips who were great sounding boards. Thank you to Brooke for her editing skills and also to Andy & Barb Lesperance; Jennifer Freeman; Mike & Brenda McDowell; Debbie Honeycutt; Janice Shivers; Venecia Liu; Sue

Stanton; Linda Schneider; Marilyn & Jack Bernstein; Kim Legleiter, Deanna Ayres; Micki Thomas; Penny Weller; Catrina Mitchell, Jodi Hobson; Molly and Tyler Lyson, Kelly Barth and Kids To Adopt in Vancouver, WA for their referrals.

I wish to thank the following people and organizations who assisted in my collection efforts while I traveled: Reverend Lyle Reece of the Central United Methodist Church in Albuquerque, NM; Betsy at The Best Western Saddleback Inn in Oklahoma City, OK; Willow Way Bed and Breakfast in Oklahoma City, OK; The Ivy Inn in Casper WY; La Maison des Papillons in Fargo, ND; Sharon of the Cathedral of Our Lady of Perpetual Help in Rapid City, SD; Foote Creek Bed and Breakfast in Aberdeen, SD; Zion Lutheran Church in Aberdeen, SD; The Spofford Inn in Kennebunk, ME; Dan Johnson of the United Methodist Temple in Beckley, WV; The Staff at Atria Assisted Living in Kennebunk, ME; Jeanne Donohue at Prospect Place Assisted Living in Keene, NH; Jules Bryant of Spartanburg Convention & Visitors Bureau, Spartanburg, SC and Sampler House Bed and Breakfast, Milton, VT.

Thank you also to Mary Skelton and Barbara Rafte of the Kent County Tourism Office, Dover, DE; Beverly Hurley from the Kansas Travel and Tourism Division, Kansas City, KS; Marla Cilley (FlyLady); Tricia Southard of the Delaware State Fair, Inc.; MacMaster House Bed & Breakfast in Portland, OR; St. Thomas the Apostle Church in Smyrna, GA; Tom Meinhold Photographer, San Luis Obispo, CA; Bruce Plotkin Photographer, Weston, CT; Mike Trompak of Timeless Images Photography, Albuquerque, NM; Barry Kaplan for his thoroughness and knowledge of the law and to Amanda Butler and Peter Honsberger who made publishing my book a lot of fun!

Thank you to Meg and Wayne of The Inn of the Tartan Fox in Swanzey, NH for providing a wonderful place to stay and being there as chauffeur and good company when my rental car broke down in addition to providing worthwhile story referrals. Also, thanks to the cooperative flight attendants of Delta Airlines who provided suggestions, referrals and/or stories. And to my neighbors, The Hughes Family, who willingly watched over my house while I traveled.

I want to specially thank all of the people who gave their stories to me whether to appease me or in hopes of having their experiences shared in a book who did not make the "cut." I hope that you can continue to share your heartfelt stories with everyone.

Printed in the United States
57389LVS00003B/17